WHAT IS MAN?

THE POWERS AND FUNCTIONS
OF HUMAN PERSONALITY

By

J. STAFFORD WRIGHT, M.A.

Principal, Tyndale Hall

THE PATERNOSTER PRESS

SBN: 85364 010 6

Copyright © 1955 The Paternoster Press
This Paperback Edition (Revised) Copyright © 1968
The Paternoster Press

AUSTRALIA:
Emu Book Agencies Pty., Ltd.,
511, Kent Street, Sydney, N.S.W.

CANADA:
Home Evangel Books Ltd.,
25, Hobson Avenue, Toronto, 16

NEW ZEALAND:
G. W. Moore, Ltd.,
3, Campbell Road, P.O. Box 24053,
Royal Oak, Auckland 6

SOUTH AFRICA:
Oxford University Press
P.O. Box 1141,
Thibault House, Thibault Square,
Cape Town

Made and Printed in Great Britain for
The Paternoster Press Paternoster House
3 Mount Radford Crescent Exeter Devon
by Cox and Wyman Limited Fakenham

WHAT IS MAN?

"WHAT is man?" is a question first recorded some 3,000 years ago, and it has grown in intensity ever since. Man is so obviously much more than a body. Mind, memory, appreciation of beauty, creative powers of thought and action—these make up the real personality. And what of humanity's powers of love and hate, that have such far-reaching consequences beyond himself? Above all, what of his sense of the supernatural, his universal consciousness of God?

In this book, the author faces these and many other questions, and marshals the evidence experience and scientific enquiry can offer. All these he tests by the Biblical revelation concerning man's nature, and the purpose of God in and for humanity. In a brief final chapter he focuses attention on the Perfect Man, Jesus Christ, in whom God came down to redeem and restore man to fellowship with his Maker.

CONTENTS

TO
MY WIFE

FOREWORD

ANYONE who presumes to write a book on such a well-worn subject as the nature of man, must make some apology in his foreword, and justify what he has done. This means, in effect, that he must say how his book differs from other books on the subject. Theologians have written fuller and deeper books from the Biblical standpoint. Students of psychology, and of what is now often called parapsychology, have written fuller and deeper books from their own standpoint. But to the best of my knowledge no orthodox Christian in recent times has attempted to examine and assess the accumulating evidence that comes from many fields; looking for any truth that may be found there; and estimating the whole in the light of the inspired Word of God.

I had felt for a long time that there was a need for a book with this approach. Then one day Mr. Howard Mudditt of The Paternoster Press mentioned that he would like to publish such a book, and suggested that I might write it. Now that it is finished, I must make it clear that neither he, nor any body of Christians with whom I am associated, is responsible for such conclusions as are found in it.

I should like to thank the Council of the Victoria Institute for permission to make considerable use of two papers that I read before them. One on miracles has been almost entirely rewritten in Chapter VII , but the bulk of the paper on reincarnation remains in Chapter XII. The section on the spirit of man in Chapter XIII was originally written for the *Life of Faith*, and is reproduced by permission of the Editor. The students of Tyndale Hall read through some of the earlier chapters in MS. form, and made some useful comments; most of their suggestions have been adopted.

One or two technical points must be mentioned. Footnotes have been deliberately omitted, and all the relevant matter and references have been incorporated in the text. After each chapter a few books are suggested for further study; these suggestions are far from being a complete bibliography, but they are books that I have found to be relevant. All quotations from the Bible are normally taken from the Revised Version, but occasionally I have slightly modernized the language without reinterpreting the sense.

It is my hope that this book will be read by those who are not yet convinced Christians, as well as by those who are. I have tried to be scrupulously fair in all that I have written about other views, and not to set up teachings out of their context in order to knock them down and score debating points. From time to time I have used an *argumentum ad hominem*, and adopted some position that is less than what I believe to be the truth, in order to meet some contention. Generally the context will make this clear; otherwise, if some remark were taken by itself, it might seem to Christians reading the book that I had departed from the faith!

J.S.W.

Bristol, 1955

FOREWORD TO SECOND EDITION

I AM glad that the demand for this book in all parts of the world has made it possible to make it available for the wider readership of a paperback edition, since there is evidence that it fills a gap in Christian literature. The opportunity has been taken to reduce the length of the book by removing much of the recommended further reading which was included at the end of each chapter of the original edition, but which has now been replaced by later publications, which are listed in the selected bibliography at the end of the book.

To avoid any increase in price, no major additions have been made to the main text of the book, although additional notes on topics that have arisen since the book was first published, such as psychedilic drugs, like L.S.D., have been included. For further information on inner world experiences interested readers are referred to a booklet that I wrote recently, *Zen and the Christian* (S.P.C.K.). Further material on Spiritualism will be found in another booklet of mine that has recently been revised (Church Bookroom Press). On the subject of Tongues, which are no longer confined to Pentecostalists, I still believe that one can find a balanced assessment in Dr. A. T. Schofield's *Christian Sanity*, an older book which I have now revised and edited in paperback format (Oliphants).

I am grateful for the wide interest expressed in this book in its original edition, and I trust that the many who have asked for it since it has been out of print, and others, will find benefit from this new revised popular edition.

J.S.W.

Bristol, *1968*

CHAPTER I

GOD THE CREATOR

SOME books on Man have missed the mark because they have not adequately recognized his relationship to God. Yet man is distinguished from the animal world by his capacity for worship and for knowing God. So at the very beginning of this book we must move back behind man himself to the Creator of man. It is of course possible that man has spontaneously evolved from some primal element, or elements, and that the idea of God is pure fiction. But such a belief has so many difficulties that it is preferable to work from the more likely hypothesis, that there is indeed a God, who is responsible for the existence of the universe in general and of man in particular. If this is so, it is impossible to consider man apart from God, unless God is merely a capricious Being; since He must have created man to fulfil a certain purpose. It is true that man might fulfil that purpose unconsciously: but it is also likely that, since man is a rational being, he is called upon to realize God's purposes deliberately.

It is not the purpose of this book to argue for the existence of God. Very few people have been led to God by the standard arguments. But those who on other grounds have had an experience of God, find that their belief in His existence can be justified intellectually through these arguments.

THE CHRISTIAN BELIEF IN TRANSCENDENCE

There are, then, two contrasting views of the Being of God. The one sees Him as transcendent, the other as immanent. The Bible holds both views together, and the Christian maintains that only so can we have a true understanding of God.

The transcendence of God appears in all those passages which speak of Him as Creator, as dwelling in Heaven, as King, as Father, and as future Judge. He stands over and above this universe of time and space, and, when men approach Him, they approach One who is other than themselves. The idea of heaven above is a necessary concept for the doctrine of transcendence. There are those who speak as though the Biblical writers imagined God as somehow spatially situated in the sky. We need not credit them with so little intelligence. Need we suppose that the psychiatrist, who speaks of the subconscious, or of the superconscious, imagines that the human mind is a house with a cellar and an attic? Yet, if we are to translate the facts of the eternal realm into spatial terms that our minds can grasp now, there is no other term that we can use of heaven than *above*. Thomas Hood tells the story of a blind man to whom someone tried to describe the colour of scarlet. The description was so good that at the end the blind man said, "I understand perfectly. Scarlet is like the sounding of a trumpet." If you think it out, is not that exactly what scarlet would be, if it were translated into terms of sound? Similarly I believe that when we do at last experience what heaven is, we shall see that we could not have grasped its nature in any other spatial terms than that of *above*.

When Jesus Christ prayed, we are told that He did so "lifting up His eyes to heaven" (John 17: 1). The early Christians followed this example, "lifting up holy hands" (I Tim. 2: 8). When Jesus finally left this earth, St. Luke, who has been proved to be a reliable historian, described how He ascended from the earth into a cloud (Acts 1: 9–11). Hence the first Christians expected Him to return in the air (I Thess. 4: 16, 17). Today it is fashionable to speak of all this terminology as *Myth*. This can be misleading, and it assumes a knowledge of reality that is no more likely to be correct than the facts which sacred history records.

By this I mean that if anyone in the body could be observed in the process of passing from this material plane to the heavenly plane, the likelihood is that the movement would be upward, and not downward or sideways. The Bible reports two instances, namely Jesus Christ and Elijah. The evidence for the former may perhaps be regarded by some as stronger than for the latter. But the critic, who talks of Myth, must in his turn suggest an alternative direction for the final departure of Christ. Certainly there came a time when, after seeing Him at intervals after His Resurrection, the disciples were suddenly convinced that they would see Him no more. What occurred to give them this conviction?

Where the Myth School is correct is in holding that the (alleged) factual records are significant, not simply as (alleged) facts, but because of their meanings. Where this School is wrong is in holding, as some do, that the meaning is valid apart from the facts, particularly when we are concerned with the life and work of Jesus Christ. The meaning of *Above* is, as we have seen, that God is not to be confused with the world-process, as pantheism suggests. The world, created by Him, has fallen from its perfection, and must now be redeemed and restored. God, in the person of Jesus Christ came *into* the world-process in order to redeem it. Christians are redeemed through the Spirit of God *coming from above* and *into* them, as Christ pointed out, when He told Nicodemus that he must be born again by the Spirit from above (John 3: 1–8). *In the New*

Testament salvation never comes by developing something that is already within, but by receiving something that comes from above. This is an important distinction, and we shall return to it more than once.

THE CHRISTIAN BELIEF IN IMMANENCE

Yet this thought of God as transcendent is only one half of the truth. The Bible also speaks of God as immanent. This thought is not expressed so strongly as is the other. Curiously enough, some Christians think it is expressed far more specifically than it really is, and in consequence they move away from the Biblical doctrine of the New Birth from above, to the unbiblical doctrine of the fostering of the Christ-spirit within. To other Christians it comes as a surprise to find it there at all, and they are puzzled about how to fit it into Evangelical theology.

The New Testament states the doctrine of immanence like this: "He (God) is not far from each one of us: for in Him we live, and move, and have our being; as certain even of your own poets have said, For we are also His offspring" (Acts 17: 27, 28). Here Paul is quoting from certain Greek ideas, but is evidently quoting with approval. If however, we consider, as some think, that Paul was on this occasion giving a sub-Christian address to win the favour of the Athenians—which I myself do not think is a likely interpretation—yet when writing to the Colossians he says of Christ, in 1: 17, "He is before all things, and in Him all things consist (or, hold together)." This is the same thought as occurs again in Heb. 1: 3, where Christ is spoken of as "upholding all things by the word of His power."

The force of these verses is that God, the Creator, is different from a human Creator. If I make a piece of furniture, its continued existence does not depend upon my own existence. When I die, the piece of furniture will still be here; my life is not in it. But, if the Bible is correct, the relation of God to the universe has in it something more. God Himself sustains the universe in existence, so that if it were possible for God to die, at that moment the universe would fall into nothingness. All existence derives—in the present tense—from Him, and exists in Him.

Perhaps we can see the difference between this idea of immanence and the idea of pantheism by a simple equation. Christianity and pantheism agree that the universe minus God = Nothing. Pantheism also holds that God minus the universe = Nothing. But here Christianity states its equation differently. To us Christians, God minus the Universe = God. In other words, to us, the Universe is not in any sense necessary for the existence of God, but God is necessary for the continued existence of the Universe.

IMMANENCE AND THE INDWELLING
OF THE SPIRIT

It commonly happens that sincere pantheists, who wish to have Christian teaching on their side, confuse two things that the Bible keeps separate. These two things are the Immanence of God, and the indwelling of the Holy Spirit, which is regarded in the New Testament as the special prerogative of Christians. A few verses from different passages in the New Testament will make it clear that the Holy Spirit is not *within* everyone, but is received *from above* as the gift of God. John 7: 39 says that the Spirit was not given until after Jesus was glorified at the Ascension. Before His Ascension Jesus told the disciples to wait for the promised Spirit (Luke 24: 49; Acts 1: 4, 5). At Pentecost the Holy Spirit came down "from heaven" (Acts 2: 2–4), and afterwards the onlookers in Jerusalem were told how they also might receive the Spirit (Acts 2: 38, 39). St. Paul repeatedly refers to the fact that Christians are those who have received the Spirit, in contrast to the people of the world, who have not received Him (*e.g.* I Cor. 2: 12–14; Gal. 4: 4–7). There is not a single passage in the New Testament which says that all men have the Spirit of God as part of their natural heritage. Yet it is no rare thing to find writers quoting verses about the Holy Spirit in the Christian in such a way as to confuse this with the sustaining life of God in all men.

How then can we make a valid distinction between the two things? Is it possible to have *more* or *less* of the Presence of God? Put in this way, it is very difficult to answer with a straight Yes or No. It would be truer to say that there are different modes of manifestation of God in His creation. This is obvious. Since there are countless varieties in the created order of animal, vegetable, and mineral, each variety needs a different method of maintenance by the Divine Being. If one says that there is one Divine life flowing through all things, and upholding or maintaining all things, this life must be different in manifestation in the rocks from what is in the plants, and different again in the lower animal world from what it is in man.

We are concerned now with man. Man maintains his existence because he is upheld by the living God. He experiences, generally without realizing it, the life-stream that flows from God. This life-stream emerges in a mind-body relationship. It enables a man to function as a human being. There was a time when "human being" meant more than it does today. Before the Fall, a human being was one who was centred in God. He was spiritual as well as mental and physical. Sin disorganized man, and cut him off from conscious fellowship with God. His spirit died, and mere existence as a human being, even though that existence depends upon God, cannot now bring the spirit to life.

We cannot do better here than turn to Jesus Christ's interview with Nicodemus in John 3. "That which is born of the flesh is flesh; and that which is born of the Spirit is spirit. Marvel not that I said unto thee, ye must be born anew (or, from above)" (John 3: 6, 7). Birth must be "of water" as well as "of the Spirit" (ver. 5). Christ was probably referring to the promise in Ezek. 36: 25-27, where the coming of the Spirit to dwell within is coupled with the sprinkling of water to make clean. If sin has cut us off from the life of God, sin must be washed away. Otherwise the incoming of the Spirit would be like putting life into the corpse of a leper without curing him of his leprosy. So before Christ finished His interview with Nicodemus, He spoke of His coming death upon the Cross, using the familiar words of John 3: 16: "God so loved the world, that He gave His only begotten Son, that whosoever believeth on Him should not perish, but have eternal life."

There are two inseparable sides to the Christian Gospel— cleansing from sin through the death of Christ on the Cross, and the receiving of a new quality of life through the coming-in of the Holy Spirit. For analysis we can separate them, but in experience we find both through putting our trust in Christ as the Saviour who carried our sins on the Cross, and by receiving Him into our heart.

The answer to our problem of distinguishing between the general immanence of God in all men and the indwelling of the Holy Spirit in the Christian, appears to be this. The ordinary man has the life-force from God to sustain him in living on this earth. The Christian is brought into contact with God through a new channel, described as the spiritual, which brings him into a personal relationship with God as Father, Son and Holy Spirit. We shall consider this further in chapter XIV.

GOD AS PERSONAL

In closing this chapter, we must have a definition of the term *Personal* as it is applied to God. Let us be clear, first of all, that we do not mean that God possesses a physical body, nor that God is a limited individual. Negatively we mean that God is something more than an unconscious and unknowable force. Positively we mean that He possesses those attributes that belong to self-conscious life. Bishop Gore defines a personal being as one who is "conscious of himself and of his relationship to all things that in any sense exist, capable of determinate will and judgment and action, and self-determined by essential spiritual character" (*Belief in God*, p. 146).

CHAPTER II

THE MIND OF MAN IN DEPTH PSYCHOLOGY

IN this chapter we shall be turning to the Psychologists for help. There are two sorts of Psychology. Academic Psychology is moving more and more towards the study of man as a machine, and to the measuring and classifying of his responses and reactions. This is a most important work, and is of great practical value in the spheres of industry, business, education, and all that goes to make up the life of man.

The other group of psychologists is engaged in the practical work of psychiatry and psycho-therapy, and generally works with an entirely different technique from the first group. In particular these psychologists build their theory and their practice upon the existence of the Unconscious, a concept which is regarded with suspicion by the other group.

Of the two groups the second is obviously dealing more closely with what we commonly mean by *Mind*, as opposed simply to the physical Brain. Most of us have an idea of an immaterial mind that is in some way related to the brain, as the pianist is to the piano. This idea has been attacked, as, for example, by Gilbert Ryle in his book *The Concept of Mind* (Hutchinson, 1949), in which he tries to get rid of the idea of the " ghost in the machine." To him the term *Mind* should have the same sort of significance as the term *Digestion*. There is no organ of our body known as Digestion, but the term is a convenient one to describe the whole process of the assimilation of our food. Similarly, there is no immaterial ghostly faculty known as the Mind, but the term conveniently describes the whole process of thinking, in the widest sense of the word.

There is a branch of psychology, known as Behaviourism, which believes that the whole of man's thinking, willing, and feeling, can be explained in terms of mechanistic responses. Man is no more than a complicated machine. The older Behaviourism has received apparent reinforcement from the modern electronic "brains," which are able to calculate and to solve problems in ways that resemble the working of the human brain. Parallels have been drawn between their responses, their difficulties, and their treatment, and the responses, difficulties, and treatment of the human brain. It is easy to forget that it is man's mind (or brain) that has invented these machines, and at the moment it does not appear likely that any electronic machine will be invented that can itself be creative, as the mind (or brain) of man is creative.

It has often been pointed out that if Behaviourist ideas are correct, there can be no such thing as truth, and no Behaviourist is ever entitled to say that his ideas are truer than any others. All that he is entitled to say is that his set of responses have acted in such a way as to lead him to enunciate Behaviourist ideas.

But side by side with attempts to get rid of the concept of mind there has been a parallel movement, based on scientific experiment, which has led to precisely opposite conclusions. These are the experiments that will be referred to in Chapter IV and V. These experiments, which seem to show that mind can function without the normal physical channels, are not necessarily relevant to psycho-analysis, though they are relevant as an answer to Behaviourism. Psycho-analysts were building their theories before these experiments were thought of. Nor must it be thought that we are tied to a view of *either* mind *or* physical brain. More and more we must keep returning to the basic fact that man is a unity. We examine different planes on which he functions, but none of these planes is the whole man. We are trying to insist, however, that no relevant investigation should be left out, and, with this thought in mind, we can turn to the psychiatrists.

Modern psychiatry has three pioneer names attached to it, Freud, Adler and Jung, and of these only the third is still alive, and still pursuing his way as actively as ever. Freudianism has followed the course of any religious movement; it has its rigidly orthodox group, its progressives, and its heretics. Strictly speaking, the term *Psycho-Analysis* is the prerogative of the Freudian School. The Jungian School has the approach known as *Analytical Psychology*, while Adler's approach is that of *Individual Psychology*.

All these groups are firmly convinced of the importance of the Unconscious. If one compares the mind of man to an island, the conscious part represents the comparatively small piece of land above water. The Unconscious is the far greater part that goes down to the bed of the ocean. The Unconscious is not simply the storehouse of the memories. Certainly it is that, and all the evidence goes to show that nothing is ultimately irretrievable to memory even though it seems to be forgotten. But also the Unconscious is the seat of the impulses, drives and neuroses, both good and bad, which are continually affecting our conduct. It is, in fact, the power-house of the life.

Readers who are already familiar with the teachings of the New Psychology, will naturally pass over the next few pages. But in investigating the mind of man, we are bound to know briefly what the New Psychology believes that it has discovered.

For Freud there are three active factors in the mind of man. (1) At the root of everything there is the ID (or, IT), which may be visualized as an unorganized mass of undirected energy, seeking expression in two main ways, the way of pleasurable satisfaction, and the way of aggression or destruction. The way of pleasure is response to Libido, which means *Desire*, and which is to be understood in terms of sex—though sex in the Freudian sense is a very wide term. The two ways of expression may be called the Life Instinct and the Death Instinct.

(2) Next comes the EGO (or, *I*). This is centred in consciousness and represents the choosing part of us, which endeavours to organize the Id in the light of reality. Yet it has to draw its energies from the Id in order to control the Id. The Id demands immediate satisfaction, but the Ego has to modify these demands.

(3) The Ego is guided by the SUPER-EGO (or, OVER-I), which is the equivalent of conscience. It is built up unconsciously during infancy, and becomes the seat of authority, sometimes of extremely violent authority.

The unfortunate Ego is caught between the wild beast of the Id and the rod-bearing Schoolmaster of the Super-Ego. Small wonder that it often evades the battle, and pushes debatable points into the cellar of the Unconscious, not deliberately (which is Suppression), but without realizing it (which is Repression). Unfortunately these repressed ideas become storm-centres below the surface, and are none the less dangerous because they are unconscious. The big ones eventually leak out or explode out, but in such a disguised form as will pass the vigilance of the Ego. For example, a sense of guilt may come out as a compulsion to be continually washing. The Ego then may pride itself on its passion for cleanliness, but the Unconscious is finding a partially satisfying substitute for cleansing from guilt. The neuroses are usually far more intricate than this, and the Psycho-therapist employs analysis to bring to the surface the repressed trouble, the issue that was unconsciously shelved and not freed. We cannot now go into the whole theory, but it must suffice to say that orthodox Freudians trace all neuroses to infantile sexual impulses that have been repressed; and their findings can be understood only in the light of their whole theory of infantile development.

Neo-Freudians, like Melanie Klein and W. R. D. Fairbairn, differ from Freud over the development of the Unconscious. They lay less stress on the Libido as the sex drive, and more stress on the building up of a good and bad object-relationship in the Unconscious.

In the first excitement that followed the publication of Freud's theories, people interpreted them as having explained away religious experience, and as demonstrating that a person can be healthily minded only if he gives full rein to his sexual desires. It is true that Freud himself wrote against religion: on his own theories this can be accounted for by his bad relations with his father. But Freudian psychology, in analysing man's mental growth and re-actions, cannot pronounce on the validity of that to which he responds. A religious man will behave in ways that resemble the behaviour of non-religious people, but the religious belief to which he responds may be either right or wrong. The idea of God may be the desire for the human father projected out on to the unseen world. But it may equally be true that the father-son relationship on earth is only satisfactorily experienced because it is a copy of the Heavenly Father-earthly son relationship. This is in fact what St. Paul suggests in Eph. 3: 14, 15, when he says, "For this cause I bow my knees unto the Father (Gk. *pater*), from whom every family (Gk. *patria*, which also carried the idea of *Fatherhood*) in heaven and on earth is named (or takes its name)."

The other erroneous deduction from Freud's teachings, namely that all sexual desires must be indulged, could bring only bondage and not freedom. Defiance of the Super-Ego brings as much misery as the defiance of the Id.

What Freud has shown is that man is disorganized from his earliest days. No one yet has built up his Ego and Super-Ego in the right way. Something is wrong at the heart of man's being, and the Christian speaks of this as original sin. Moreover Freud has shown how many troubles are due to a repressed sense of guilt. Not long ago we were told with some satisfaction that modern man no longer bothered about his sins. In the light of the New Psy-chology—even apart from the Bible—we are bound to say, "So much the worse for modern man."

It would probably be true to say that most practising psychia-trists today, Christian and non-Christian, make use of the basic Freudian ideas, even though they may not be thorough-going Freudians.

In a paper read before the Victoria Institute in 1951, under the title of *A Preface to Biblical Psychology*, Dr. Ernest White attempted to link up some Freudian terms with their Biblical equivalents. He compared the Id to the animal *Soul* of Scripture (Heb. *Nephesh*; Gk. *Psyche*). The Biblical *Heart* includes the functions of the conscious mind, and also the conative elements of the Unconscious, *i.e.* the impulses that rise from the Unconscious into the Ego.

Alfred Adler is the second of the Big Three, but it does not seem as though he has had the following of the other two. His chief contribution was his interpretation of man in terms of a drive for power, and it is to him that we owe the idea of an inferiority com-plex. Incidentally, most people use this term in the wrong way. It does not really mean a conscious feeling of inferiority, but rather an attitude of somewhat overbearing authority which issues from an unrealized sense of insecurity, as when the little man "throws his weight about."

Jung is undeniably the most exciting of the three to the religious man, if the religious man is also an introvert. The extrovert would probably have little sympathy with him. With those two words we pass straight into Jungian thought. Jung classifies men and women into these two basic types, which are not precisely the same as introspective and extrospective. They describe ways of reacting to life. The extrovert has the positive approach to life, accepts facts as facts, and fits or misfits easily into his relationship with people and events. The introvert has the negative approach, prefers ideas to facts, and does not find it easy to drop into place in company.

But each of the two types may function in one, two, or even three, out of four possible ways. Generally one is emphasized more than the others, and one or two are dormant. The four functions are as follows:

(1) THINKING. This term denotes the rational and logical approach. The extrovert thinker is concerned with facts, objective data, and formulæ. The introvert thinker is concerned with working out the ideas behind the facts, and may become the type of the absent-minded professor.

(2) FEELING. This is the opposite to thinking, and is concerned with emotional reactions and values. The extrovert-feeling type prizes right relationships, and can be sympathetically helpful. The introvert-feeling type has deeper emotions, but tends to satisfy his emotions in æsthetic pursuits, such as poetry and music, or the more colourful types of religion.

(3) SENSATION. This type lives by sense-perceptions, and tends to take experiences as they come, without pondering over them, or drawing up any scale of values beyond the intensity of the experience. They may be the easy-going, jolly sort, but may degenerate simply into pleasure seekers. The extrovert pursues the objects that cause the sensation. The introvert dwells upon the sensation itself, and the object becomes secondary, as often happens with the productions of modern art.

(4) INTUITION. By this word Jung intends to indicate that the reaction comes *via* the Unconscious. The extrovert of this type is the adventurer, who continually guides his life by chances and "hunches," while other people are waiting for some logical certainty before acting. The introvert intuitive is an adventurer in the inner world of ideas, particularly the inner world of his own Unconscious. He may become a religious crank.

After writing this analysis of the types, it seemed a good idea to try to set out a possible response of each type to a notice outside

a shop, "Ice-cream sold here."   I have not submitted this to Jung,
so I must accept responsibility if I am wrong!

(1) THINKING.

Extrovert.   "I wonder what the formula is."

Introvert.   "What makes people buy so many ice-creams these
days?"

(2) FEELING.

Extrovert.   "They sell X's ice-cream here.   It's much' nicer than
Y's."

Introvert.   "Beautiful texture this ice-cream has! and don't you
like the shape of the tubs?"

(3) SENSATION.

Extrovert.   "Oh boy!   Let's go in and buy one!   What couldn't
I do with an ice!"

Introvert.   "How cold it is!   And how cold my heart has grown
lately!"

(4) INTUITION.

Extrovert.   "I haven't any money, but I'll see what a smile
will do!"

Introvert.   "There is a purpose in my seeing that notice just now.
How does it fit into the plan of my life?"

Obviously it is rare to find a person who comes entirely under
one of these heads.   But we all tend to move in one or two of
these directions.   Self-knowledge should result in a greater toler-
ance towards people of other types from ourselves, and a realization that, for a full-orbed personality, we shall endeavour to bring
out into the light those opposite sides of our nature that are in the
darkness.

To Jung the self is an exciting thing.   It displays certain characteristics, but it is continually reminded of the opposites that go
to form it.   It is both conscious and Unconscious, and from the
Unconscious there flow the forces that can help towards the indi-
viduation of the self.   Jung differs from Freud by holding that the
Unconscious is not simply the battleground of infantile repressions,
but is itself pointing the way towards wholeness.   Thus the
Jungian interprets dreams not only in terms of the repressed past,
but in terms of the way-out for the present and future.

Moreover, Jung believes in what he calls the Archetypes of the
Collective Unconscious.   The idea of a Collective Unconscious
may sound absurd, but since it links on to other things that we shall
say concerning the nature of man, it will be a good thing to try to
make it clear now.   In the Unconscious there lie, as one would
expect, the experiences, ideas, and reactions, that the individual has
personally experienced.   But in the treatment of some patients
Jung found ideas and pictures emerging in their dreams and drawings that were similar to ideas and pictures of days gone by, and that

appeared to be similar in meaning for the patient. Sometimes such ideas might have been picked up years before and forgotten, but at other times it was virtually certain that they were previously unknown to the patient. Jung therefore postulated a pool of ideas that was common to the human race, or, from another point of view, a racial way of responding to facts and ideas.

If this can be accepted, it at once links up with the underlying unity of the myths of all nations. The hero, the dragon, the quest for the treasure, the consequent sufferings, the witch, the good fairy, the winning of the bride—all these are basic themes. Moreover, how often have the peoples of the world felt a significance in the rising and the setting of the sun, the coming of the spring, the reaping of the harvest, and the oncoming of winter; a significance that is more than physical, and that calls for a mythological and ritual response. So we have, for example, the myths of a dying and rising God. Jung refers to these basic pictures as Archetypes.

Not long ago it was fashionable to produce these myths as parallels to some of the Christian stories, with the implication that the Christian stories also were fictitious folk tales. Quite apart from the historical vindication of the facts of the birth, crucifixion, and resurrection of Jesus Christ, it is not difficult to see how Jesus Christ fulfilled in the sphere of history these deep longings of the human heart that had previously found their outlet in bare mythology.

The theologians who are now engaged in demythologizing the Bible may be treading on dangerous ground. Granted that there is a theological use of the term "Myth" which does not equate it with "Fairy tale," yet, if Christianity is only effective as myth that must be translated into concrete terms, then it is difficult to see how it is superior to any other myths that tell of dying and rising Saviour-gods. The historical facts of the crucifixion and of the bodily resurrection of Christ are vital for New Testament thought.

In yet another way the demythologizing school may be on dangerous ground. The "myth" of which they speak cannot be translated into matter-of-fact science without serious loss. Here Jung is absolutely correct. There is that in man which cannot be satisfied with the purely scientific approach. The revival of interest in music and the arts is only to be expected in this technical age. So also is the growth of the mystical approach to life. When the ministry of the Word of God becomes the Ministry of Religious Technology—and this danger is becoming a real one—then the heart of Christianity will have gone. But let us be clear; we are not asserting the primacy of vague religious mystery, but the need for an intelligent response, based upon both historical and eternal facts. We must be able to express ourselves in the language of today, but the human mind may respond better to the age-old symbols than to the concrete structures of modernity.

But to return to Jung—it has probably become clear, even from this very incomplete treatment of some of his ideas, that he holds a much more dynamic theory of the Self than does Freud. In Dr. White's paper, already quoted, he finds a link between the Biblical teaching on the spirit of man and Jung's idea of a larger consciousness (though it is unconscious to us) which is aware of all the processes of the living organism, which is man. We shall be discussing more fully the nature of spirit in chapter XIV.

What then may we gather about man from the New Psychology? Clearly the mind of man is a complex system. It is more than a machine for thinking and remembering. It has vast depths that can best be pictured as a power house from which the Ego derives its capacity to live. The source and nature of the power is wrapped in mystery. To some extent the power house is wired-up by the Ego, but much of the wiring is done without the realization of what is actually in progress. As a result, dangerous connexions are made, and the power sparks and burns at these connexions, and from time to time flashes out, sometimes disastrously.

There is a certain waste of power also, since the Ego tends to use it for very limited ends, whereas there are other systems built up in the power house that should be brought into operation to produce full orbed personality.

"Who then can be saved?" This question, asked by the disciples in a different connexion, is what any intelligent person must ask here. For the moment it must be sufficient to say that the New Psychology has confirmed the fact—if it needed confirmation—that the Gospel of Salvation must deal with the heart, and not simply with surface morality; for it is from within that the sins of man come out. One is reminded of Christ's words to this effect in Mark 7: 20-23. Secondly, the New Psychology has shown the need for an inner controlling centre, and Jung has indicated that there may be depths (or heights) in the Unconscious that go beyond the limits of the individual self. Could this be where spirit makes contact with God? Thirdly, the New Psychology has shown that man must bring as much of himself as possible out into the open. This is particularly important where sin and guilt are concerned; and Christianity places the confession and removal of sin in the forefront of its Gospel.

CHAPTER III

MAN AND HIS BODY

FROM the speculations about the unseen mind of man we pass to the very tangible body. Here at least we feel on familiar ground, with something that a plain man can understand. But the moment we listen to some real authority talking on the body, we realize how little we plain men really know. A previous book in the *Second Thoughts Library*, written by Professor A. Rendle Short, whose study of the human body extended over a lifetime, was entitled *Wonderfully Made*. The words come from Psa. 139: 14, and the microscope, and the dissecting scalpel, confirms them. The more we know, the more we marvel.

The component chemicals and elements of the body can be separated, weighed, and valued. Their market value before the war was about 2/6. Doubtless they are worth more now. Yet these chemicals and elements grow together into a living machine that surpasses imagination in intricacy. But in one moment the mysterious life-force may be cut off, and from that very second the glorious machine begins to disintegrate into its dead component chemicals. It returns to the dust to which it belongs (Gen. 3: 19).

We cannot here discuss in detail theories of the evolution of man's body. There are certainly large gaps in the fossil evidence, and it is difficult to postulate sufficient time for the gradual evolution of the human body and its component parts from a unicellular form of life to its present state. It may well be that there were a number of sudden creations, in which there were many basic similarities with previous and contemporary forms of physical structure. This is the method that we employ in our own inventions, and it can be illustrated from the evolution of the aeroplane. The bird did not beget the jet plane through cross-breeding with a motor-bike, nor did it develop rudimentary propellers on its wings, but, since both bird and plane are made to be at home in the air, there are certain similarities between them, even though the motive power that drives them is different. Similarly, if the links between modern man and the so-called hominids are not yet found, it may be that they do not exist, but that at a certain point of time God created a new being, and gave him a body that was structurally much the same as the body of the apes and the hominids that walked on two legs, but that differed in mental, and especially in spiritual capacities. However, we are concerned with man as he is now, and any readers who believe that the evidence for the evolution of man from a one-cell creature is convincing, need not leave this chapter unread.

The Body-Mind Relationship

Man, then, is a creature with a physical and material body. There are many things about the relationship of the component parts of this body that the wisest do not yet understand. For example, in recent years much has come to light about the influence of glands upon man, and here we see the close linkage between the physical and the mental. Under-activity of the thyroid gland, for example, makes for slowness of movement and slowness of understanding. Over-activity makes for high tension and drive. Over-secretion of the pituitary seems to be linked with courage and initiative, while under-secretion is linked with lassitude and timidity.

Many mental illnesses are now being treated by physical means. There is the insulin shock treatment, which is sometimes effective in schizophrenic illness. There is also an electric shock therapy, which produces an effect similar to an epileptic fit, and which is often effective in relieving depression: it has been suggested that the electrical therapy is effective because it stimulates the pituitary gland in the skull beneath the brain. Again, there is the surgical operation of pre-frontal leucotomy, in which the nerve fibres between the frontal lobes and the rest of the brain are severed. The value and ultimate success of this operation are still much disputed, but certain cases of overwhelming depression have been entirely relieved after the operation, though a spirit of irresponsibility may supervene.

This new knowledge can be exploited in terrible ways when physical means are used to batter down the doors of resistance to some ideology. Simple "truth drugs" pale into insignificance before some of the methods that are reported to have been used to extract confessions from political prisoners. In some cases it would seem that the results have produced, not merely a confession through fear, but a genuine rearrangement of mental ideas comparable to a "conversion" (cp. p. 139).

Yet over against the influence of the body upon the mind, one must set an equally strong influence in the other direction. Mental outlook has a decided influence upon physical health, and a bad letter by the morning post often upsets us for the day. It is not often that an opportunity comes to study this scientifically. But a book, *Human Gastric Function*, by Harold G. Wolff and Stewart Wolf (Oxford University Press) contains the interesting story of

"Tom" and his stomach. Tom was an employee of the New York Hospital, who had a physical disability which necessitated his being fed through an opening in the wall of his stomach. The two doctors therefore were able to study the effect upon his stomach of emotional disturbances. When they deliberately made him angry, the lining of his stomach became congested, and bled at the slightest touch. In such a state the stomach is liable to become ulcerated. Depression produces a grey stomach, covered with mucous, and tends to result in chronic gastritis. Other parts of the body also are affected directly through right and wrong thinking.

This must make us think of the Bible attitude to health. Health is often promised as one of the blessings of obedience to God. Thus there is a promise to Israel in Deut. 7: 15, that, in response to obedience to God's commandments, "the Lord will take away from thee all sickness." In James 5: 14, 15, healing through anointing with oil is connected with the confession and forgiveness of sin. This obviously does not represent the whole truth: the story of Job stands in the Bible as a warning not to assume that illness is always the result of personal sin. There are various causes of illness; but, looked at from the positive standpoint, it would be true to say that an attitude of quiet dependence upon God, that produces peace at the centre, is the seed-bed for a normally healthy life. And a depressed, angry and vicious attitude of mind will tend to produce some sort of illness in the body.

THE USE OF THE BODY

Nothing more will be gained here by discussing further facts about the constitution of the body. The question that naturally rises is, "Now that I have a body, what am I to do with it? What is the purpose of it all?" There are three possible views that one can take of the place of the body in the life of man. (1) That it is the prison-house of the soul. (2) That it is the only part of man that counts; and so let us eat, drink, and be merry, for to-morrow we die. (3) That it is the "partner" of the soul, the expression of the Ego, and the means of glorifying God and growing in the true life.

One thing is obvious: a material body is necessary for any creature that is to live in this world, so far as we can tell. Angels and spirits do not live "in this world," in the usual sense of the term. Before Christ could live in this world, He was born with a human body. If then, God has created us with material bodies, it must be so that we can live as an integral part of this material world. He has made us of a different type from angels and spirits. This would seem to tell against the first view, that the body is the prison-house of the soul. The Greek philosophers mostly held this, and the mystic commonly tends towards it. It is a view that generally has an ennobling effect on a man's life, unless it leads him to withdraw from all real contacts with his fellow men.

Even orthodox Christians may drift into the prison-house view if they confuse the earth and the "world"—to use the latter term in the special Biblical sense. A Christian is to be separate from the world, from which he has been called out (*e.g.* John 17: 16; James 1: 27), but on the other hand "the earth is the Lord's, and the fulness thereof" (I Cor. 10: 26), and God "giveth us richly all things to enjoy" (I Tim. 6: 17). A definition of "the world," would be, *That form of life which is organized on the assumption that all values are bounded by the horizons of birth and death.* Nothing counts except the things that can be touched and seen. The difference between Christians and "the world" should be seen in the way in which they handle the things of the earth. A Christian, for example, should regard money as a trust, to be used in the light of eternal needs. His standards of getting, spending, and saving, are different from the standards of the world. He may shed many of his responsibilities by giving his money away, and perhaps living a celibate life in a community. But otherwise he will have to spend his money in the light of the fact that he and his family have material bodies that need food, work, and recreation, as well as being those in whom the eternal life of God dwells.

The second view of the body, that it is the whole of man, need not keep us long. In general it has a thoroughly bad effect upon a community where many of its members adopt it as an easy-going philosophy of life. When held as a creed, it does not always have the practical effect that one would expect. There are many avowed atheists who have high moral standards, though it is true that they often hold somewhat lax views on sex and marriage. Communism is the chief representative of this materialistic view in the world today, and probably this will be the rock on which Communism will eventually founder, since the denial of the supernatural is so difficult for man.

The third view of the body is the Christian one; by this we do not mean that it is held only by Christians, nor even that all Christians hold it. But it appears to tally with the New Testament conception.

When we first considered this question, we put it in the natural form, "What am I to do with my body?" In other words, we made a distinction between an Ego, or I, and my body. We feel that there is some sort of relationship between an inner and an outer *Me*. The body is the expression of myself in relation to the world of time and sense. It is *I* living in the world. If therefore, for purposes of analysis, we make a distinction between an Ego and a body, we must regard the relationship as one of partnership. The body is not my master, to govern me according to the imme-

diate demands of the senses.   Nor is it my enemy, which must be
maltreated and broken.   It is the sole means that I have of glorifying
God in this world, just as it is the sole means that an athlete has of
winning the race.   As partners we shall need to follow the athlete's
practice of discipline and denial; yet denial will not be an end in
itself, but only a means to an end.

Again one must draw a distinction between the body and the
"flesh," in the Biblical sense, just as we distinguished between the
earth and the "world."   The flesh in the New Testament is always
regarded as something to be resisted and crucified.   The new life
of the spirit is constantly at war with it (*e.g.* Gal. 5: 16–25).   A
definition of the "flesh" would be: *Life organized round the idea of
the gratification of the physical senses.*   That is to say, the unifying
factor in life becomes self-gratification through the channels of
the body.   Christians and non-Christians alike are bound to live
through the channels of the senses: the difference should be seen
in the way in which the sense impressions are used and organized.

In I Cor. 6: 13, Paul, singling out one aspect of the flesh, sums
up the matter when he says, "The body is not for fornication, but
for the Lord; and the Lord for the body."

But the body is not inherently sinful.   If it were, Jesus Christ, the
Son of God, could never have been born into the world as He was.
Nor would the Christian be told to present it to God as a living sacri-
fice (Rom. 12: 1), since sins cannot be given to God for Him to use.

A Christian, who sees the truth about his body, can never despise,
abuse, or maltreat it.   His body is the temple of the Holy Spirit
(I Cor. 6: 19), and a temple is a place where God manifests His
presence.   His body is the instrument that God has given to him
so that he may glorify God in this world, and so that he may consequently grow as a whole man.   The Ego cannot grow apart
from the body in this world: it must grow in and with the body, and
it is "the things done in the body" that are the subject of consideration at the judgment-day (II Cor. 5: 10).

There is one necessary exception, which is not really an exception,
to these general statements about the treatment of the body.   A
Christian naturally does not neglect his body; but he may be called
to live a life that involves physical hardship.   On the pioneer
mission-field he may deliberately face situations in which his health
is likely to be damaged and his life shortened.   He will be doing
only what Paul himself did, and in his turn suffering the list of bodily
hardships that are listed in II Cor. 11: 23–27.   The reason why
this is not really an exception is that every Christian life is to be
guided by the particular call of God.   Length of life is not the
measure of faithfulness of service.   In obedience to the call of
God there lies the pathway to the development of the whole personality, whether the life be long or short.   The Ego must see the

plan, but the Ego must carry out the plan in the body. The body is the gift of God to be an essential part of man's whole being. "Glorify God therefore in your body" (I Cor. 6: 20).

ADDITIONAL NOTE ON HYPNOTISM

Several times in this book I have referred to hypnotism, without saying anything about its nature. In a way this is not surprising, since no one yet knows what exactly it is. We know that it produces a heightened suggestibility, and varies from a comparatively light state to a deep cataleptic state that can be produced in only a small proportion of people. The electrical activity of the brain, as registered on the electroencephalogram, is, the same as in the unhypnotized state; the rhythms do not change as they do in sleep.

Under hypnosis a subject will accept suggestions made by the hypnotist, and can be induced to endure physical strains of which he would not normally be capable. Unless he is told that he will remember what has happened when he comes round, he will be unaware of what he has said and done during the deep state of hypnosis, though he will remember it again if he is subsequently rehypnotized. Under hypnosis he can be told to perform a certain action directly he comes round, or at some given time afterwards; and he will do this at the appropriate time; if the action is ridiculous, he will often give some sort of explanation for doing it.

Hypnotism should never be exploited as a parlour game, but a qualified man can often use it to help sufferers of one kind or another. The danger of its use is that in removing some nervous symptom through hypnotic suggestion, or alleviating a pain, the hypnotist may not be getting to the real root of the trouble, and may in fact be covering up some disease of which the pain is a warning symptom.

There is some evidence that hypnosis has occasionally released clairvoyant powers, but this is probably in people who already had these powers in a rudimentary form; it does not happen with most subjects.

In 1948 I heard a most interesting lecture by Dr. William Brown, who in the course of his life hypnotized hundreds of patients. He stated that he had come to employ hypnotism less and less, and suggestion during complete relaxation more and more. He found that the latter process linked the suggestion with the total personality, and made for a more effective cure.

A sane and interesting book is *Hypnosis: its meaning and practice*, by Eric Cuddon (Bell, 1938).

CHAPTER IV

THE MIND AND SPACE

So far we have seen something of how the mental life of man is linked to the functioning of the body, including the brain and the glands. We have also tried to see the mental life from the standpoint of New Psychology, which has disclosed a whole area of the mind that is normally unconscious. Those of us who accept the idea of a Mind at all, undoubtedly have a picture, or at least an idea, of some tangible thing that resides in the head, and that extends its influence just so far as the physical body can reach with its limbs or perceive with its senses. Thus, if my wife in the armchair opposite to me shows me a picture, my mind, through my sense of vision, perceives what the picture is. If the room is badly lighted, or if she holds the picture at an awkward angle, or if I am not wearing my glasses, my mind may get an erroneous idea of the picture, though I shall certainly perceive some of the objects in it. Or suppose I am playing Snakes and Ladders with my youngest boy, and have won the first game. It seems only fair that he should win the second, but unfortunately I am leading, and a throw of six with the dice will get me "home": on the other hand a "one" will land me on a snake, which will take me almost back to the beginning. My mind, having decided on losing, can produce a "one" by a little manipulation of the dice with my hands. Often my mind can go further afield than my own room. It may, for example, perceive events that are happening in Australia, when I pick up one of the Australian radio stations on the short-wave, and television may rush me from one end of the country to the other in a moment of time. Yet in none of these instances has my mind functioned except through physical channels. The mind lives in the house of the body, and never goes out on its own.

Probably this is the sort of picture that we have of our minds. It is so true to experience that, as we have seen, some people think that it is the whole truth, and that it is gratuitous and superstitious even to postulate anything like an immaterial mind, when man can be explained simply in terms of a reacting physical brain.

There has, however, always been a strong body of belief that, on occasions at least, the mind can reach out beyond the walls of its physical house. Stories of telepathy and clairvoyance go far back into the past. They are to be found in the stories of most of the nations of old. They are to be found at the present day, and it is almost impossible to raise the subject in any gathering of friends without someone relating a tolerably authentic story, and saying, "Well, how do you explain this?" The sceptic invariably demands more evidence, and this usually creates a difficulty. It is normally impossible to furnish the cast-iron evidence that the sceptic demands; even when reasonable evidence is available, it is always possible to fall back on the "explanation" of coincidence.

What is needed is some test of telepathy and clairvoyance that can be reproduced under rigidly controlled conditions like any other scientific experiment. No scientist could then ignore these tests without being an obscurantist, and, if the tests are positive, one must admit the existence of something that is not in the least explicable by the laws of physical science. The only reasonable conclusion would be that there is something in the nature of an immaterial mind, that can make contact with other minds and objects without the use of the senses or of the nervous mechanism that characterizes physical communication. In other words, pure materialism will have received a mortal wound.

The only way of evading this conclusion would be to say that these things will ultimately become explicable by physical laws: but this is an act of faith for which there is no warrant. Certainly a reasonable person will see that such experiments as we have postulated would tend to support the traditional Christian, and even non-Christian, belief, that there is something in man over and above his brain and physical body. Of course, this cannot prove Christianity, nor can it become a new Gospel of salvation. But it puts the burden of proof upon the materialist. It is for him to show that in spite of these discoveries he can still honestly remain a materialist.

But all this rests upon a "suppose." We must now see what experiments have in fact been devised in what is now known as Parapsychology, and how far they can be regarded as convincing. It is usual to refer to these faculties which form the subject of study of Parapsychology as the PSI (Ψ) faculties. At the moment we are concerned chiefly with Telepathy and Clairvoyance.

TESTS FOR TELEPATHY AND CLAIRVOYANCE

Telepathy is the transference of knowledge from one mind to another without any contact through the physical senses. Clairvoyance is the awareness of objects or objective events without any contact through the physical senses. If you become aware of my thoughts when you are not in physical communication with me, that is telepathy. If I shuffle a pack of cards, take one out, and put it face downwards on the table without myself or anyone else knowing what it is, then, if you have become aware of what it is, that is clairvoyance. But if I, or anyone else, can know what the card is, then it will be impossible to tell whether your awareness is the result of clairvoyance from the card, or of telepathy from our minds. And, as we shall see, there is another factor, that of possible precognition, which makes it extremely difficult to tell whether such awareness is clairvoyance, or telepathy, even if no one at the time knows what the card is. Cards are a useful means of demonstrating the truth or falsity of alleged telepathy and clairvoyance. The transmission of drawings where the receiver endeavours to produce a picture at which the sender is looking, is difficult to assess. Unless there is a succession of accurate drawings, it is not easy to decide how to score the attempts, though a matching system has been devised to deal with this. With cards the receiver is either right or wrong, and the judge is not dependent upon his subjective opinion.

Of course, very great precautions must be taken. Those who have heard the Piddingtons or Maurice Fogel on the wireless know what an amazing display of telepathy can be given by highly competent stage methods. Fogel admittedly is a stage telepathist, and the Piddingtons have never offered themselves to be tested under control conditions by serious psychical researchers.

Experiments must take place under rigid test conditions, so that it is absolutely impossible for the receiver to make physical contact with the sender or with the cards. In the experiments to which I shall refer, it is absolutely certain that these conditions have been fulfilled. The next thing of which we must be sure is the method of scoring. Normally results will not on the face of them be spectacular. If they were, there would be no need to devise the experiments at all, since telepathy would by now be an obvious fact. What we must know is the number of cards that the receiver is likely to guess correctly by chance alone. If then he tells correctly more than the chance expectation, there may be a case of extra-sensory perception, or ESP. We say, "may be," because obviously one run through the cards with a score above chance would prove very little. The chance expectation is not so fixed as that. But statisticians are able to give tables and figures that will enable one to say how far above or below the chance expectation any figure is for a number of runs through the pack. Here again the experiments to which I shall refer have been scrutinized by mathematicians. At the Annual Meeting of the American Institute of Mathematical Statistics in 1937, an official statement was made that, "Assuming the experiments have been properly performed, the statistical analysis is essentially valid. If the Rhine investigation is to be fairly attacked, it must be on other than mathematical grounds" (J. B. Rhine, *The Reach of the Mind*, p. 132. Faber, 1948). In spite of this, Dr. Spencer Brown of Oxford has recently attacked the methods of computing the chance factor in these experiments. He has written several articles in *Nature* and has broadcast his views in the B.B.C. Third Programme. I am afraid that his theories of randomness are beyond me, as I am not a mathematician.

If cards are used, an ordinary pack of fifty-two playing cards is not the most suitable type, and would create difficulties in assessment. If, for example, the receiver said, "Seven of clubs" and the card was the seven of diamonds, how many marks should he receive for guessing seven? Or if the card was really the seven of spades, should he receive more marks, inasmuch as he guessed the correct colour of the seven?

Hence we must have a pack of cards that can be simply assessed. In practice the cards used are known as Zener cards, or ESP cards. A pack consists of 25 cards, composed of 5 sets of 5 different symbols. There are 5 each of a cross symbol, a circle, a rectangle, a star, and two wavy lines. If a receiver attempts to guess the order of these symbols in a pack of 25, chance alone would give him the expectation of 5 successes. If he consistently scores more than 5, statisticians can say what the probability is that chance alone did not produce the result.

From 1930 onwards experiments of this kind have been carried on in Duke University under the direction of Professor J. B. Rhine. The results of these experiments have been published from time to time, and may conveniently be assessed in Dr. Rhine's book *The Reach of the Mind*. The records of every single experiment have been published, or are open for public inspection, so as to avoid any accusation of having boosted up the figures by publishing only the favourable results. Moreover, although some receivers were obviously better than others, Dr. Rhine has worked with all types, though he has generally drawn his subjects from the students in the University.

In 1934 when the total results to date were analysed, and when all the bad receivers were included with the more successful ones, the average for more than 3,400 runs through the pack was 7 per 25. This may sound small, but since a series of only 6 runs with an average of 7 would be significantly above chance, it is obvious that the same average for 3,400 runs is of very great significance. If we turn to some individual scores, the above-chance figure mounts tremendously. One man averaged 8 per 25 for more than 700 runs through. To express the odds against a similar result by chance alone would, as Rhine says, require a paragraph of figures.

There have been times when a receiver scored 9 correct hits in succession, and a few days later scored 15 in succession. A child of nine, who on one occasion made up her mind to get a perfect score, so as to win a prize that was offered, was successful with all 25, as was also a sixteen-year-old boy. Cases of this kind seem to me to outweigh the objections of Dr. Spencer Brown.

All this laboratory work sounds dull, and the results that it has produced seem almost negligible. But its importance is that it has put such things as telepathy and clairvoyance upon a scientific basis. Once this is done, one can pass on with greater freedom to more spectacular cases, and, while we shall do our best to obtain cast-iron evidence for each case, we should now be prepared to approach the subject with a more open mind.

Spontaneous telepathy or clairvoyance is often associated with some emotional crisis, particularly with illness or death. A typical case is that of Mrs. Bettany, quoted in *Phantasms of the Living*, by Gurney, Myers, and Podmore (Vol. I, p. 194). When she was a girl she was walking along a country lane when she suddenly saw, imposed upon her surroundings, a vision of a certain bedroom in her house, with her mother lying on the floor, apparently dead. She was so convinced of the reality of what she had seen that she ran at once to the doctor's house, and brought him home with her, though she was unable to answer the detailed questions that he put to her, since, when she had left home, her mother had been perfectly well. Her father was amazed to see her arriving with the doctor, but, when they went to the bedroom, they found the mother lying on the floor exactly as she had appeared in the vision. She had collapsed with a heart attack, and the doctor's speedy arrival saved her life. In the vision the daughter had even noticed a lace-bordered handkerchief lying beside her mother, and this was there as she had seen it.

Many cases of this type can be studied in *Phantasms of the Living*, and in a further collection of cases by Mrs. Henry Sidgwick, published in 1922 in Vol. XXXIII, Part 86, of the *Proceedings of the Society for Psychical Research*. But, leaving these aside, it is probable that many people experience simple examples of telepathy in their daily lives. One member of a family is often aware of something that has happened to another member before the news has come by ordinary means. This is frequently the case with identical twins.

One most successful series of experiments in telepathy was conducted by Professor Gilbert Murray as the "receiver" and some member of his family as "transmitter." (*Proceedings S.P.R.*, Vols. XXIX and XXXIV). While the Professor was out of the room and out of earshot, the transmitter told the other friends in the room what he or she would concentrate upon. On returning to the room Professor Gilbert Murray was frequently able to discern what the subject was, with a considerable degree of accuracy. To quote one example: the transmitter thought of Rip Van Winkle coming down the mountain. Professor Murray reached the solution as follows: "Oh, I've got this. It's an old sort of gnome-like person with a matted beard coming down—very funny feeling expecting to be known and find things—Oh, it's Rip Van Winkle."

POSSIBLE EXPLANATIONS

In this chapter we are deliberately keeping to the range of the mind in space, and hence are omitting any reference to the foreseeing of the future. But, so far as space is concerned, it would seem that we are wrong in picturing the mind as being confined to the walls of the physical body. There are occasions when it can become aware of people and events by non-physical means. We may call this Telepathy or Clairvoyance, but to name a thing is not to explain it. Various hypotheses have been suggested, but none has met with general acceptance.

The suggestion that the brain sends out something akin to radio signals is an attempt to give a physical explanation. Certainly electrical waves are now known to be sent out by the brain, but the striking thing about telepathy is that it is not apparently affected by the distance of the transmitter from the receiver. All physical types of energy fall off in their intensity inversely as the square of the distance from the source. Moreover it has been pointed out that the physical transmission of an idea from one brain to another demands a code—whether words or symbols: but in telepathy no such code exists, unless we are to suppose that each person is born with an unconscious awareness of such a code which can be used to build up words or pictures in the mind.

But if we rule out any purely physical explanation, we are left with two possibilities. (1) If we accept the fact that the immaterial mind of Mr. X can affect or control Mr. X's own physical brain, it may be that Mr. X's immaterial mind can also on occasions affect or control the physical brain of Mr. Y. Since we do not know how our minds are connected with our physical brains, we cannot dismiss the possibility of some connexion with the physical brains of other people. This is briefly the theory of R. H. Thouless and B. P. Wiesner expounded in the *Proceedings of the S.P.R.*, Vol. XLVIII, p. 177 (1947). (2) We may suppose that the immaterial mind of Mr. X can make direct contact with the immaterial mind of Mr. Y. Mr. Y only becomes aware of this connexion when his own immaterial mind puts into his physical brain the information or picture that it has received from Mr. X.

The latter is roughly the underlying idea of Whately Carington's theory, which he has set out so fully in his book, *Telepathy* (Methuen, 1945). It is impossible to do justice to his theme in a brief summary, but the basis of his belief is that, just as two ideas become associated in a single mind so that the mention of one will bring the other to mind, so the presentation of one of these ideas to another mind will tend to make the same associated idea appear to that other mind also. In other words, there is a certain linking of individual minds at a subconscious level. Quite obviously, there is very much more to it than this bald statement, since for 99.9 per cent of our daily lives we appear to be individuals in mind and in brain. But the fact that we are not aware of a subconscious linkage does not prove that such linkage is not a reality.

The subconscious is essentially unconscious, and we find it hard enough to recall our own ideas and memories when we wish, let alone the ideas and memories of other people. But undoubtedly there are people who have gifts of telepathy and clairvoyance that they can exercise almost at will, and they may well be those who are able to perceive the contacts that their subconscious mind has made with the subconscious minds of others. We shall see the importance of this when we come to consider the subject of Spiritualism.

OPERATIVE LAWS

Meanwhile it may be as well to note down some of the laws that appear to operate in Telepathy and Clairvoyance.

1. PSI faculties work best when some emotional or interest factor is involved. If a participant in a test is bored, he is likely to produce results of little positive significance.

2. Probably it is for this reason that statistics indicate that normally the most significant results with the card tests occur at the beginning and end of a session of tests. This may also be the reason why people with a known gift of clairvoyance do not do well on the card tests: they cannot raise much enthusiasm for such a dull thing as guessing the order of cards.

3. Drugs affect the capacity to score in tests. Large doses of Sodium Amytal, which make the subject drowsy, reduce the capacity to score above chance. Alcohol in large doses has the same effect. Caffeine, on the other hand, increases the capacity to score (J. B. Rhine, *The Reach of the Mind*, pp. 102, 103). This reminds us that we are dealing with a mind-body relationship, and would be accounted for by supposing that the drugs, in acting on the physical brain, affect its capacity to perceive the messages from the mind.

4. Concentration is normally a hindrance to success. If a test can be treated more as a game in a happy atmosphere, it is more likely to produce significant scores. Rhine mentions the effect of hypnosis in this connexion (*Reach of the Mind*, p. 103). Hypnotized subjects scored better when they were given the suggestion

to treat the test as a game, and lower when told to concentrate hard. It is evident that in the tests to which Dr. Rhine refers the suggestion was given under hypnosis, but the test was carried out after the subject had returned to the normal state.

5. Confidence normally produces better results than scepticism. Rhine mentions some of the "sheep and goats" experiments of Dr. Gertrude Schmeidler (*Reach of the Mind*, p. 118). The "sheep" are those who are favourably inclined to ESP, the "goats" are the sceptics. The "sheep" score consistently higher. Sometimes the "goats" score very much lower than the chance expectation. The interesting thing about this is that the subconscious minds of the "goats" must presumably be aware of the correct cards, but deliberately produce a low score: in other words, their well-below-chance average is too good to be true!

6. The evidence of tests would appear to show that the receiver is very much more important than the transmitter. In clairvoyance naturally the receiver is 100 per cent responsible, but where two or more people are involved, as in telepathy tests, a good receiver can usually produce results with any transmitter with whom he, or she, is on good terms, though there are occasional exceptions. On the other hand I have not seen any evidence to suggest that there are star transmitters, in the sense that they can increase the good results of any average receiver.

The same fact probably holds good for spontaneous cases. In the case of Mrs. Bettany, for example, it seems more likely that the girl was largely responsible for the vision than that her unconscious mother acted as a strong transmitter, especially since the girl had somewhat similar experiences on other occasions, when apparently her mother was not involved. Moreover, in most cases where someone becomes aware of another's danger or imminent death, the transmitter is not aware of any telepathic message going out from himself. It does not follow that no message does go out. But where there is some vision of the person in danger, it usually appears from the standpoint of a spectator and not from the standpoint of one who is undergoing the experience. In other words, it is more as though the receiver is transported to the scene than as though the transmitter is sending out an SOS describing his condition.

Nonetheless it would be foolish to make a hard and fast rule of this, since undoubtedly people have, both consciously and unconsciously, transmitted an impression of themselves to someone else. A striking example of this is the case of Mr. & Mrs. Wilmot, related on p. 100. Further, the facts of Psycho-Kinesis, which will be discussed in Chapter VII, show that people have capacities for the powers of transmission of thought-force. If we ask what exactly is transmitted and received, there is no single answer.

Sometimes the receiver sees a picture or a vision, sometimes he receives an impression or an impulse. He does not know how the impression comes, generally he cannot make it come, and almost always he is unable to say for certain whether the impression or vision is entirely accurate, or whether it is partially true and partially false.

8. Rhine's experiments show that the majority of people possess PSI faculties to some slight degree. If this is true, it has a bearing upon several things in the Christian life, particularly upon prayer, upon the unity or disunity of any body of Christians, and upon the influence exerted by a preacher.

ADDITIONAL NOTE

In this chapter I have referred to some of the more important books. Those who are familiar with the subject will notice that I have not attempted to draw out detailed distinctions between Telepathy and Clairvoyance. I have done this deliberately so as not to overload the chapter.

Fortunately the distinctions do not appear to have much practical significance, since with few exceptions, receivers obtain approximately the same proportion of results with either telepathy or clairvoyance.

In this chapter I have deliberately omitted any Biblical references so as not to introduce at this stage any idea of the supernatural. For example, one might quote Elisha, who repeatedly told the king of Israel of the secret plans made by the king of Syria and his Counsellors (II Kings 6: 8–12). This could well be an example of ESP, but a Christian might say, "This was not a natural faculty at all: God revealed the plans to him." The same could be true of some of the telepathic perceptions of Jesus Christ, as, for example, the coin in the fish's mouth (Matt. 17: 27), and his words to Nathaniel (John 1: 48). Were these altogether Divine perceptions, or did He, as Man, possess perfectly those faculties that all perhaps possess in rudimentary form, and that some possess to a heightened extent? For the moment we must leave these questions unanswered, though we shall return to them later. Meanwhile, we note that no one has the right today to dismiss such stories out of hand as unlikely fables or legends.

For a cogent criticism of Dr. Spencer Brown (p. 44), see *Modern Experiments in Telepathy* (p. 349 f), by S. G. Soal and F. Bateman (Faber, 1954).

CHAPTER V

THE MIND AND TIME

ONCE we had a universe consisting of three dimensions of space, and with a time-scale neatly divided into past, present and future. Now modern physics has given us a space-time continuum. Most of us do not understand in the least what this means, and, if "understand" means "form a mental picture of," one supposes that not even Einstein understood it. At the best it is a mathematical conception that accounts for certain facts in a way that the older conceptions failed to do. But it is of no practical significance whatever.

The ordinary man, however, has always believed that time is not quite as simple as it appears. It is all very well to have the three neat divisions of a non-existent future, a no-longer existing past, and an experienced present. But how can we account for the capacity of the human mind on occasions to foresee the future? The obvious answer is, "It can't!" But the obvious answer has turned out to be wrong.

TESTS FOR PRECOGNITION

Once again proof has come from the dull statistical methods employed by Dr. Rhine and others. The story has often been told, but it will bear telling again. In this country Dr. S. G. Soal spent many hours trying to reproduce Dr. Rhine's experiments with cards, but with disappointing results. The scores showed little deviation from the chance expectation. Meanwhile Mr. Whately Carington, who had been conducting picture tests for telepathy and clairvoyance, thought that some of his subjects were reproducing pictures that were to be "transmitted" at a future date and missing the present picture. He therefore suggested to Soal in 1939 that he should go through his records of card guesses (128,350 of them), and see whether any of his 160 receivers were guessing significantly above chance for the card immediately preceding or immediately following the card that was actually being transmitted.

Dr. Soal undertook this immense task, and discovered that two of his subjects were obtaining significant results with the following card. On testing them again he found that one, Mrs. Stewart, was now hitting the target card significantly above chance, while the other, Mr. Basil Shackleton, was continuing to score on the next card to be turned up.

At Duke University other tests were made for precognition. In guessing the cards in the pack two main methods had been used. In one the receiver guessed the cards as the transmitter turned them up; naturally the two people were completely cut off from communication with one another. In the other no transmitter was employed at all, but the receiver, as we may continue to call him, had a pack of Zener cards on the table in front of him, and, without touching them, recorded the order in which he believed them to be from the top to the bottom of the pack. Only when he had finished his series of guesses was the pack examined and checked against what he had said.

Adapting this latter method, Dr. Rhine suggested that the receiver should try to guess what the order of the pack would be when it had been shuffled a certain number of times. This meant that he would be guessing an order of cards that did not exist at the time of his guess and that was not known to anyone at all at the time. In order to eliminate the human factor as far as possible, the packs were shuffled mechanically. Yet under these conditions the receiver continued to guess significantly above chance, giving odds of 400,000 to 1.

Other experimenters in Britain and the United States have since devised other tests for precognition, and precognition is now accepted by many serious students as an attested fact. So once again, as with telepathy and clairvoyance, one may move with greater confidence from the statistics of cards and pictures to the more interesting cases of prediction.

NOSTRADAMUS

There have, of course, been some remarkable examples. Some of the most spectacular are the prophecies of Nostradamus. Michel de Nostradame was a Frenchman and a Hebrew Christian (Roman Catholic) who was born in 1503. He was trained as a doctor, and appears to have been extremely competent as a medical man. His fame, however, rests upon his book, known as the Centuries, of which he published several editions from 1555 until his death in 1566.

This book consists of sets of four-line verses, written in French, Latin and doggerel, and in these verses Nostradamus claimed to foretell the future up to the year 2000 A.D. The most accessible book for studying him is *Nostradamus*, a biography by James Laver (originally published by Collins in 1942, and republished by Penguin Books in 1952). Some of the predictions are so startling that the casual reader may wonder whether there is something "fishy" about their publication, and whether they were really touched up after the event. This was my own impression at first, so I spent an afternoon in the British Museum Reading Room consulting an edition of the Centuries dated on the title page 1605, and found that the verses really do stand there as they are quoted.

The quatrains of Nostradamus usually appear to be obscure and nonsensical. Nostradamus claims that he deliberately made them obscure, because otherwise the civil and ecclesiastical leaders of the day would be likely to condemn his predictions, when they found many things in them that did not suit their own ideas. As a result one gathers the impression of a great deal of dross, amongst which gold can be found from time to time.

Nostradamus, who died in 1566, undoubtedly foresaw the French Revolution in 1789. We take, as a striking example, the quatrain IX, 34.

> Le part solus mary sera mitré:
> Retour: Conflict passera sur le thuille
> Par cinq cens: un trahyr sera tittré
> Narbon: et Saulce par coutaux avons d'huille.

Laver translates this as follows on p. 151:

"The husband alone will be mitred. Return. A conflict will pass over the tiles by five hundred; a traitor will be titled Narbonne; and from Saulce we have oil in quarts."

We may disagree with small details of this translation, and the 1605 edition has slight differences of punctuation; but the main words are not in dispute. The first two lines could refer to the mob who invaded the Tuileries and compelled Louis XVI to wear the red cap of liberty, which was not unlike a mitre. This may not sound very convincing. But when we come to the two names, we are bound to take notice. The Comte de Narbonne was Louis XVI's War Minister, who was intriguing with the revolutionaries, and so was justly named "a traitor." The other man was actually named Sauce. He was the Procureur of Varennes, who arrested Louis XVI on his attempted flight: he was by trade a grocer and chandler. Carlyle in his *French Revolution* describes the incident; "Alas, alas! Sieur Sausse, Procureur of the Township, Tallow-chandler also and Grocer, is there, with official grocer-politeness."

Parallel predictions of equal significance will be found in Laver's book. Naturally the more obscure verses have been a happy hunting-ground for all sorts of interpretations, many of which have been disproved by the course of events. But it seems that Nostradamus foresaw aerial warfare when he wrote (V. 8):

Sera laissé feu vif, mort caché,
Dedans les globes horrible espouvantable.
De nuict à classe cité en poudre lasché
La cité à feu, l'ennemy favorable.

Laver translates again (p. 229):

"There will be loosed living fire and death hidden in globes,
horrible! frightful! By night hostile forces will reduce the city to
powder, the fact that it is already on fire being favourable to the
enemy."

PREDICTIONS IN THE BIBLE

Predictions of this kind have never been taken seriously by
theologians. The writer has spent a great deal of time on Old
Testament study and lecturing, and one of the most exasperating
experiences has been to find commentators and writers rejecting
out of hand the predictions of the Bible. It is an axiom for many
modern commentators that a definite alleged prediction must have
been composed after the event, and the prediction becomes a
criterion for dating the section or the book; or the prediction is
treated as a later addition. Examples are such passages as the
Blessings by Jacob in Genesis 49 and by Moses in Deut. 33; the
forecast of exile and return in Lev. 26; the naming of Josiah in
I Kings 13: 2, three centuries before he came, and the Book of
Daniel.

At the risk of becoming obscurantist I would also include the
second part of the Book of Isaiah. Traditionally the whole Book
of Isaiah is by Isaiah, the son of Amoz, who lived in the last part
of the eighth century B.C. But in chapters 40–55 there is a change
of atmosphere; the writer appears to have the Babylonian exile in
mind; and he even names Cyrus as the deliverer in 44: 28 and 45: 1.
Because of these two facts, the chapters are commonly ascribed
to a writer, or writers, towards the end of the exile, when Cyrus
was appearing on the horizon as the great conqueror. He ultimately captured Babylon in 538 B.C. Yet even a casual reading of
these chapters will show that time after time God, through the
prophet, is declaring that He can predict the future, and He chal-
lenges the idols to do the same. Many of the "idols" could have
made a good guess that Cyrus would capture Babylon once he was
rising to power. Here, if anywhere in the Bible, one would expect
some startling prediction, written long beforehand to show that
God had taken even the exile into account and had not forgotten
His people. A writer, criticizing this view, said that it does not
matter to us whether the chapters were written by Isaiah or by
someone else. That may be partly true: but it certainly mattered

to the people who first read it and for whom it was first intended. It is, of course, a fact that the atmosphere is that of the exile, yet the examples of psychometry, which we shall be looking at shortly, show that, in seeing "visions" of the future and of the past, the "seer" often seems to be living in the scene described, and feeling the emotions belonging to it. That this is also a characteristic of predictive prophecy is clear from such passages as Jer. 4: 19–31, where Jeremiah virtually experiences the future invasion of which he speaks. Moreover Isa. 40–55 contains such remarkable descriptions of the Lord Jesus Christ that, to be consistent, one should date these chapters A.D. rather than B.C.!

This digression is not intended as an attack on all modern theologians. Some of them are already realizing that the findings of psychical research have a significance for Biblical study, but they have not yet seen clearly the significance of the fact of detailed precognition. The possibility of precognition does not *automatically* mean that every alleged prediction in the Bible is true: other factors may enter in. But it does mean that every alleged case should be most carefully weighed before it is rejected. More will be said about this when we consider the nature of prophecy.

SEEING THE FUTURE

Prediction today is usually connected with gipsies and fortune-telling. To the writer it seems undeniable that gipsies and others have gifts of foreseeing the future, whatever methods they use. It is arguable that the external methods, whether concentration on the hand, crystal, tea-leaves or cards, may serve the purpose of relaxing the normal consciousness, and thus releasing the sub-conscious powers of prevision, which in these people are retained by a thinner dividing wall than in normal men and women.

One might illustrate this by a parallel from one of the standard psychological tests known as the Rorschach Test. In this test the person is shown in succession twelve standard patterns that were originally made by ink-blots. Some of us used to make patterns of this kind at school. You fold a piece of paper down the middle, and on one side put blobs of ink or paint close to the centre crease. Then you quickly press the paper together, and squeeze out the ink as far as it will go. When you open the paper you find a symmetrical pattern, with the same design reproduced on both sides of the crease.

The Rorschach Test uses twelve standard patterns of this kind. The person is confronted with one, and then describes what picture or pictures he sees in it. The assessment of the results is a highly skilled task, but the Test gives a remarkably good assessment of the personality and its tendencies. The reason is that the pictures that are seen are largely born in the subconscious mind, even though the conscious mind elaborates them. Pictures in the fire, or pictures in the clouds, are seen in much the same way, but of course they lack the standardization of the Rorschach blots.

Now when a person has a latent gift of prevision, the picture seen in the tea-leaves, or in the hand, or in the crystal, can take on a precognitive character. It unlocks the gate of the subconscious, and sometimes the key turns very easily in the lock.

Apart from professional fortune-tellers, the gift of second sight, as it is often called, is found more frequently among certain races than among others. On several occasions the Skolt Laplanders have been in the news, and talks have been given about them on the radio. An appeal was made to supply them with new reindeer, which form their means of livelihood, since they lost most of their herds during the war. Those who have lived among them say that their powers of telepathy and prevision are highly developed, and they are said to use telepathy to make appointments to meet one another.

In the British Isles, the Scots, Welsh, and Irish tend to possess the gift. There is an interesting study by Lewis Spence in *Second Sight: its History and Origins* (Rider, 1951). He is concerned particularly with the existence of the gift in Scotland, and gives many examples drawn from different centuries, with a good review of the literature of the subject. Mr. Spence believes that the earliest reference to second sight in British literature is in the *Polychronicon* (I. lxiv), of Ranulph Higden, written about the middle of the fourteenth century. Higden says concerning people in the Isle of Man; (I have modernized the spelling); "There oft by daytime men of that island see men that be dead toforehand, beheaded, or whole, and what death they died. Aliens set their feet upon feet of the men of that land, for to see such sights as the men of that land do." The last sentence refers to a belief that persisted in Scotland, that the seer could communicate the vision to another if the other made contact with him by standing on his feet.

Towards the end of the seventeenth century John Aubrey carried out an investigation of second sight in Scotland, and included his findings in his *Miscellanies* in 1696. He obtained much of his material by the questionnaire method, and in the eight questions that he sent out he included two that are of special interest here: "If the Second Sight be a thing that is troublesome and uneasy to those that have it, and such as they would gladly be rid of?" "If any person, or persons, truly godly, who may justly be presumed to be such, have been known to have had this gift or faculty?"

One reply says that the gift is certainly troublesome, and most people who have it would like to be free from it. Its possessors were mainly virtuous, but scarcely godly. Another reply is from a minister near Inverness. He agrees that the gift is troublesome, but says that godly people frequently have it, though they regard it as something sinful, proceeding from the devil. Sometimes public prayer has been made for their deliverance, and this has been effective.

Certainly ministers have possessed the gift. Lewis Spence includes a section on a famous seer, the Rev. John Morrison, who was minister at Petty, in Inverness-shire from 1759 until 1774 (Chapter XII). Stories about him concern prophecies of coming events including the imminent deaths of members of his parish.

PRECOGNITIVE DREAMS

To what extent may you or I, who do not possess any gift of second sight, expect to have a glimpse of the future? There is a probability that some of our dreams are precognitive. This was strongly maintained by J. W. Dunne, who in 1927 published his fascinating book, *An Experiment with Time* (1st and 2nd editions published by Black, subsequent editions by Faber & Faber, including a cheap edition in "Q Books"). Dunne had the idea that his dreams were composed of future elements in addition to past elements, and he began to keep a careful record of all his dreams. The records confirmed his beliefs, and certainly the cases that he records are most striking. A more recent book, less seriously written, but regarded by investigators as significant, is, *Tell Me the Next One*, by John Godley (Gollancz, 1950). John Godley records seven dreams that he had between 1946 and 1949 in which he read, heard, or saw the winners of certain horse-races. Ten horses were concerned in all, including one of whom he had never consciously heard, and eight of them did actually win. There is not the slightest doubt that Mr. Godley told some of the dreams beforehand to several friends, and that he and others in consequence put money on the horses and won their bets.

Since reading Dunne's book I have often noticed precognitive elements in my own dreams. Sometimes I have told someone else the dream beforehand, but generally there is simply my own word for it, and a critic can say that I was suffering from *Identifying Paramnesia*, whereby, on meeting some occurrence I have a false memory of having experienced it in a dream. Psychologists link this with the experience of *Déjà Vue*, in which one has the feeling that one has done something before.

But I remember one outstanding example of several years ago, when I dreamt that I saw a child playing with a Yo-Yo. The Yo-Yo craze was long since dead, and I had not seen one for years. Yet next day in another part of Bristol I did see a little child playing with a Yo-Yo: and after that I did not see another for months, or it may have been for a year or two.

Someone whom I know well has occasional precognitive dreams. She is the wife of a clergyman, and, when her husband was considering a new post, she dreamt of a large white building, with pillars at the doorway, and a passage basement below, and with a pile of planks, barrels, and other rubbish lying outside the front door. When she went there she was welcomed in her dream by a Mrs. E, whom she knew slightly. As her husband was considering a teaching post at a College, which she had never seen, I asked her to describe to me the dream-building before she went to see this College. The description tallied with the College except for the planks and rubbish. Moreover her first impression on meeting the Principal's wife was, "She reminds me of Mrs. E." After they had been at the College for some months, she came up the drive one day to find that the contents of the basement, that had been used as an air-raid shelter in the war, were being cleared out, and the planks, barrels and rubbish were lying beside the doorway ready to be carted away, as she had seen them in her dream.

It is not often that a dream of the future is as clear as this. What seems likely is that future elements go to form the ideas of a dream just as past elements do. For example, if I had dreamt of the Yo-Yo on the night after I had seen the child playing with it, no one would have doubted that the actual (past) event influenced my dream. But it may equally be maintained that the actual (future) event influenced my dream.

We remember only a small part of our dreams, as can easily be proved. Have a pencil and paper by your bedside, and the moment you wake up, start jotting down words or phrases that will remind you of the dream you have just had. Then take each word or phrase and elaborate the picture. As you do so, keeping your mind as relaxed as possible, you will frequently find fresh dreams coming back to you. Record the salient points of these too. When you pick up the paper again a few hours later, you will be surprised to find how many of the incidents have already passed out of your mind. Probably one reason is that dreams are often an outlet for the Unconscious, and the Conscious mind either refuses to "own" them or else is uninterested in them. That is why, if you are looking for precognitive elements in your dreams, you will almost certainly need to write down your dreams as soon as you wake. The writing will also serve as evidence up to a point, but, if you have a dream that you believe to be precognitive, the best thing to do is to write it down and post the paper at once to some reliable person, or to the Society for Psychical Research, so as to provide positive proof when the dream comes true.

RETROCOGNITION

One could go on quoting examples of precognition, and further cases will be found in the books mentioned at the end of this chapter. But we must also take notice of possible cases of Retro-cognition, or moving backwards in time. The most famous case, which is by no means closed, is that of the two ladies who appear to have stepped back from 1901 to 1789 when walking in the Gardens of Versailles. Their own account is to be found in *An Adventure*, by C. A. E. Moberly and E. F. Jourdain. The book has run through four editions and many reprints since it was first published in 1911. The present publishers are Faber and Faber. Originally these two ladies assumed pen-names, since the story was a strange one, and they held important positions in which they did not wish to be made to seem ridiculous. Miss Moberly was the first Principal of St. Hugh's College at Oxford, and Miss Jourdain was at first Vice-Principal under her and then her successor as Principal.

There is no reasonable doubt that both ladies believed that they had had this experience, and well-known researchers have accepted the experience as genuine. Nonetheless there is just enough doubt to make it possible to reject the story as having unwittingly grown out of some vague normal experience. The second edition of the book, published in 1913, and now very difficult to obtain, contained the verbatim accounts as first written by the two ladies independently in 1901. These accounts are omitted in other editions, and, having looked through them myself, I must admit that these original accounts are very much simpler than the later. Mr. W. H. Salter has pointed out some significant differences in an article in the *Journal of the Society of Psychical Research*, Jan.–Feb., 1950 (Vol. XXXV, p. 178), and the whole story was "debunked" by J. R. Sturge-Whiting in *The Mystery of Versailles—a complete solution* (Rider, 1938).

On the other hand, W. H. W. Sabine in the *Journal of the American S.P.R.* (Vol. XLIV, p. 48), and G. W. Lambert, in the *Journal of the S.P.R.*, July–Oct., 1953 and following numbers, believe that the two ladies had a genuine experience in shifted time, though each of these writers gives a different interpretation of the experience.

One is bound to mention these differences of opinion to avoid a charge of ignoring the evidence, but on the whole I feel that, even if we allow for the touching up of some of the experiences, the two ladies did actually step back in time.

After all this preamble we come to the actual case. The two ladies went to the Gardens of Versailles on an August afternoon in 1901. As they tried to find the Petit Trianon, they saw buildings and scenes, and walked by paths that existed in 1789 but not in 1901. Although the place must have been filled with sightseers, they saw only nine people, and several of these were dressed in out-of-date clothes. At the time they had little or no knowledge of the Gardens of 1789, but they afterwards undertook an intensive research into available records, and discovered that the things that they had seen corresponded with the things that were there in 1789. They even came to believe that they had seen Marie Antoinette herself. Even though the fuller accounts contain fresh elements that were not in the original brief descriptions, one has the impression that we are dealing with two ladies of high intelligence, who are genuinely bewildered as they compare notes, and try in vain to find again in 1901 and 1902 the things that they had seen when they walked in the Gardens on that August afternoon.

Those who know of Miss Moberly only as joint author of *An Adventure*, should read the account of her life in Edith Olivier, *Four Victorian Ladies of Wiltshire* (Faber, 1945). She was a remarkable woman and a fine scholar, with an intense suspicion of spiritualism, and inclined to snub people who tried to draw her out on her own psychic experiences. Nonetheless she did tell her close friends of several other visions of the past and of the future that can be compared with the vision at Versailles, and that involved her in considerable research to check what she had seen. Her character and life must certainly be taken into account in assessing the credibility of her Versailles story. Those who are interested in old "superstitions" may care to note that Miss Moberly was a seventh child of her parents and Edith Olivier implies that she was also the seventh of a seventh. Such a person is commonly supposed to have gifts of second sight. A radio talk by Miss L. Iremonger on April 25, 1954, gave the interesting information that she was actually descended from Peter the Great of Russia.

PSYCHOMETRY

Before closing this chapter, we must mention the evidence of Psychometry. This is the term that is commonly applied to denote the exercise of a certain unusual faculty, and it was apparently first used in the middle of the last century by a professor of anthropology named Buchanan. A person with the faculty of Psychometry can take some object, and, after handling it, can disclose facts about the people who have handled the object, or who have been closely connected with it. The facts that are seen may concern the past, present, or future, of the person concerned.

The great book on the subject is by Dr. Eugene Osty. Published originally in French in 1922, it was translated and published in England in 1923 as *Supernormal Faculties in Man: an experimental study* (Methuen). **Dr. Osty was a medical man, who gave many** years to the study of what he prefers to call *Metagnomy*, using for the purpose several different sensitives. He employed them in various ways, doing his best to check their statements. In particular he kept a regular check on his own future as it was foretold by these different people. Dr. Osty's work is regarded as accurate and reliable, and his findings throw light on several points that we are discussing in this book. It is particularly significant that Dr. Osty emphatically rejects the spiritualistic hypothesis, and obtained as equally startling revelations through those sensitives who were not mediums as he did through those who believed that their super-normal knowledge was communicated through discarnate spirits.

Some sensitives worked under hypnotism, others in a waking state or very light trance. Having handled an object, they generally needed some guidance as to which particular person they were to speak about. For example, if they were given a folded letter, they might begin to describe the person who had received the letter, and Osty would have to tell them that he wanted information about the writer.

The book is a large one of 242 pages, packed with documented examples and conclusions. It would be futile to attempt any sort of summary, but a few significant conclusions should be noted.

- (*a*) Once an object had been touched, it would seem as though a contact was made with the person who had handled it, and made at a level that involved a realization of some of his past, present, and future.
- (*b*) The object itself evidently did not hold, as it were, an imprint of events, since events that had happened since the person last handled the object were known as well as those that had happened before he handled it.
- (*c*) The near future (say up to a year) was commonly seen more clearly than the more remote, and in a number of cases a most detailed prediction or description was given, which later proved to be correct. But true predictions were also made some years in advance.
- (*d*) The past or future that is seen is that of the individual who is being described. The sensitive apparently has no general knowledge of future events. Thus Osty was conducting some experiments before the outbreak of the 1914–18 War. The sensitives said nothing about the war in general, but described wounds, death, trench-digging, and other things which would shortly affect the person concerned.
- (*e*) The errors of prediction are also significant, and sometimes the wishes and plans of a person were taken up and spoken of as true, and woven into a future picture that was not realized.

(*f*) Some sensitives give a broad general view of a person's future, while others prefer precise details of individual events.

(*g*) It often happens that the sensitive seems to feel the experiences of the person whom he or she has been describing: that is, the atmosphere is, as it were, reproduced to some extent.

(*h*) The event or character described usually comes to the sensitive in a form that needs to be translated. Thus, in giving a name, one sensitive said, "I see in the family circle of this gentleman a young girl . . . a crown appears . . . stephanos (this is the Greek word for *Crown*, and the sensitive knew Greek) . . . Stephanie . . . Fanny . . . she is called Fanny" (p. 144). Dr. Osty, however, appears to go beyond the evidence of his own examples when he suggests that the sensitive does not actually see the scene as it is in reality. One thinks of the notable example on p. 104 f., when the sensitive describes the course taken by an old man who was missing from home, and sees the exact place where his body is lying. In particular she sees a large rock nearby, whereas in actual fact this proved to be an uprooted tree stump that looked like a moss-covered rock from a short distance away.

(*i*) Small details about a person are often revealed that are unknown to Osty or to others present at the time, but that are found to be perfectly correct. This is significant in considering the argument of spiritualists in similar cases, that, since a fact is unknown to anyone at the seance, it must have been revealed by spirits.

(*j*) One sensitive at least was able to reproduce verbatim on a later occasion the exact words that he had said when he was speaking of a person. The words returned to him "under the form of large printed letters that he has the sensation of reading as one reads a book" (p. 78). One is reminded of the action of Jeremiah, as recorded in chapter 36 of his book. He was able to dictate to his secretary the prophecies that he had spoken during the previous twenty years, and, when the written copy was destroyed by the king, he was able to reproduce them again.

We may conclude with a sentence in which Dr. Osty sums up his own conclusions: "Every human being knows his own entire life according to laws that are still to be discovered, and Metagnomic subjects are psychic instruments of variable quality that reveal what each human being knows concerning himself without being aware consciously, or even subconsciously, that he has this knowledge" (p. 185).

Assessment of the Evidence

We may well end this chapter in a state of bewilderment. What are we to make of this mind of man which can travel both in space and in time without these limitations that we commonly suppose to belong to it? And what becomes of our division of time into past, present and future? If the future can be known, does it already exist? And if it does, have we any freedom of choice at all?

To attempt an answer to the last question first of all: When a psychometrist (or anyone else) describes the past, we do not suppose that the actors in the event had no freedom of choice at the time. Similarly the description of the future does not mean that the actors in the future event will have no freedom when the time comes. One frequently quoted case (*Proceedings of the S.P.R.*, Vol. XI, p. 497) concerns a lady's vivid dream of her coachman falling from his box on to his head. Next day the lady in her carriage saw her coachman sway, and called to a policeman to catch him. He did so, and, by breaking the sequence of the dream, saved the coachman's life.

One may note here a difference between types of prediction. A fortune-teller commonly foretells the future without making moral judgments upon it. Predictions in the Bible usually have a moral condition attached or implied. The key verses in this connexion are Jer. 18: 7-10, where God says that when He pronounces evil against a nation, He will stay His hand if the nation repents: similarly a promise of blessing will be revoked if a nation then turns to evil.

But the whole question of the nature of time and of our passage through it is too intricate to try to solve here. Dunne has his theory of Serialism, which involves a series of "observers," in the mind of man, each with his own time-scale, and each seeing the full span of time through which the observer below him is travelling "moment by moment." One needs to be a mathematician to comprehend this theory properly. H. F. Saltmarsh in his book *Foreknowledge* (G. Bell, 1938) suggests that the present moment is not completely momentary, and that the subconscious has a wider field of "present" than has the conscious mind. The difficulty is that some events have been seen so far in advance that it becomes meaningless to bring them within the bounds of the present.

Most writers with a religious outlook fall back upon the idea of an Eternal Now, and Christians commonly speak of God as knowing the end from the beginning, and as viewing all things in an eternal present. Although some modern theologians have criticized this, and have even suggested that God may be surprised by events, yet our glimpses into the future suggest that the orthodox idea may well be true.   And it is possible to hold the idea without denying our freedom of action.

From the practical standpoint, retrocognition will undoubtedly operate at the Judgment Day, when, as the Bible says, "the Books are opened."   And if the past still exists as a living thing, it is possible for God to blot it out, as He promises to do for those who come to Him through Jesus Christ, whose blood cleanses from all sin (I John 1: 7).   And, after all, the Cross of Christ, which happened in history, looks both backward and forward in its scope.

God, then, has set man in the time process.   He is a creature of time.   And yet the facts that we have seen in this chapter show that man also trancends time.

APPENDED NOTE ON THE DROWN MACHINE

A possible extension of the principle operative in psychometry is seen in the claims that are made for The Drown Homo-Vibro Ray Therapy.   This is based on the belief that "every separate part of the human body has its own individual rate of vibration," and that "all diseases have their vibratory frequencies—slower and heavier than those coming from healthy tissue."   An appropriate machine can measure these vibratory rates, and can thus diagnose disease.   The treatment consists, so far as I can discover, in retuning the vibrations by means of this machine, though homœopathic medicines are also used.   The astonishing thing is the claim that "a blood specimen, however old, is always in resonance with the body of origin, and that an accurate analysis of a patient's condition can be made from his or her blood, and the appropriate treatment broadcast back, no matter what the distance may be between patient and instrument."   These quotations are made from a leaflet issued by a practitioner, who certainly obtains results.

If these claims be true, there are two points of special relevance for this book.   1.   The blood spot appears to be the psychometric object, conveying information about its owner, even when it has ceased to be part of his body.   I wonder whether the diagnosis of the disease is due, not to the machine, but to psychometric powers possessed by the user. Could anyone learn to use the machine?   The treatment given may also depend upon the practitioner's possession of healing powers.   Such powers will be discussed in Chapter VIII.

2.   The claims bear a remarkable resemblance to certain aspects of witchcraft where blood, nails, spittle, etc. are taken to cast a spell on their owner.   Certainly the practitioners have nothing at all to do with evil of this kind; they are concerned solely with healing and with doing good.   But it seems as though they are directing to good ends the powers that are used to evil ends by unscrupulous people.   If the one is possible, the other may be equally possible.

There are other machines for which somewhat similar claims are made, including the well-known Black Boxes of Mr. de la Warr. Readers who are interested in the contents of the boxes will find a scientific investigation in the *Journal of the Society for Psychical Research*, Vol. 41, No. 707. March 1961.

CHAPTER VI

THE SIGNIFICANCE OF BEAUTY

IT is difficult to find a comprehensive title for this chapter. We want to discuss the æsthetic activity of man, and try to discover the springs of that inspiration that comes to the artist, the poet, the musician, and probably to many others in pursuits that may at first seem remote from the æsthetic side of life.

THE ANIMAL WORLD

Is it safe to assume that a sense of beauty belongs to man and not to the rest of the animal world? One cannot count the display of birds and mammals at courting times, since the colours and the behaviour evidently act as a trigger to set in motion a series of reflex actions in the opposite partner.

Bird song also belongs to a similar category: however beautiful it sounds to us, the response of the female, or another male, to the song is not apparently based upon an appreciation of its beauty.

E. G. Boulenger writes in *Animal Mysteries* (Duckworth, 1927) of some experiments made with an orchestra at the Zoo. Some animals appeared to dislike music of all kinds; others appeared to like some. Most of them disliked tunes in a minor key. Crocodiles, scorpions, and spiders especially were attracted, while seals enjoyed everything except jazz. Boulenger has an interesting comment on snake charming, when he says that no snake evinces the slightest interest in music of any kind. The movement of their head is due to their fencing for an opening to strike as the charmer himself sways to and fro.

It has been fashionable to describe the actions of the animal world in terms of reflex responses, and there is no doubt that this is in the main correct. But it may be that there is rather more to it than that, and such books as Len Howard's *Birds as Individuals* (Collins, 1952) must make us go over the ground again.

In point of fact we simply cannot visualize the animal's world at all. Most mammals are colour-blind and see everything in black, grey and white. Birds are colour-blind at the blue end of the spectrum, but sensitive to infra-red. The hive bee's perception of colour is exactly the opposite to this. With many animals a whole new world exists because of their acute sense of smell.

Others can hear sounds that we cannot hear. Therefore to attempt to pronounce finally upon the æsthetic sense in animals is somewhat rash. Maybe a dog, who sees nothing in a sunset, is a connoisseur of smells, and finds them æsthetically satisfying.

WHAT IS BEAUTY?

Omitting, however, these "maybes" and "supposes," we are on safe ground in saying that the appreciation of beauty is one of the outstanding marks of man, and this appreciation is almost certainly one of the points in which man's likeness to God appears. To the Christian it is axiomatic that God has made the world so beautiful because He delights in beauty, and is in fact the source of all beauty. Scientific interpreters sometimes forget this, and, in trying to force everything into the strait-waistcoat of utility, miss the simple explanation that these things exist because they are beautiful.

This does not mean that everyone appreciates beauty, nor that everyone agrees on standards of beauty. 'The sense of beauty is innate, in the sense that it is there to be developed. But it may lie dormant, it may be crushed by material interests, or it may be perverted. In this way it resembles the conscience and also the perception of truth. Goodness, truth and beauty, in fact, form a trio that ultimately elude scientific analysis. They may be thought of as steps that lie between the world of physical science and the personal knowledge of God. Because they are higher than materialism they often become the final goal of men and women who find the wells of materialism running dry. If these people do not also pass to the spiritual realm, the good has become for them the enemy of the best. In our own day we have seen a revival of interest in cultural pursuits. They offer a means of rising above sordid materialism and the perversion of scientific discoveries for the destruction of mankind. This is all to the good. But beauty by itself is not the final goal for man. The wholeness of beauty is to be found in God alone.

But what is beauty? Perhaps it is safer to try to define what an appreciation of beauty is, rather than beauty itself. It is a sense of appreciation, or of exhilaration, caused by the mind's response to sights or sounds in which everything is "just right." This is not proposed as a final definition, because the "just right" is much too vague. Nonetheless it probably conveys what most of us mean by an appreciation of beauty, and it is wide enough to include both a butterfly's wing and the neat and perfectly-timed movements of the football player. It also links beauty to truth and goodness, in which also there is a feeling of "just right."

In giving this definition we have returned to the concept of mind as distinct from brain. We visualize the brain as the reception centre for the senses. The mind handles the materials that come in. It may choose to concentrate upon the physical impressions, and refuse to look beyond the things that can be touched and seen, weighed and measured. That is the way of the physical sciences. Or it may accept the fact that physical science does not show us the whole world. The analysis of the laboratory is not the last word: it needs the vision of the mind to make it complete.

It may seem rather tedious to be introducing the Unconscious again, and perhaps it looks as though it is being made the scapegoat for too great a burden. But it is difficult to see how one can propound a theory of beauty without bringing in the Unconscious. The vision of beauty in the world around us is something that cannot be reduced to those analytical terms that belong to conscious logic.

The same thing is true in measure of those who produce things that give æsthetic satisfaction. The artist, poet or musician, has his rules, and his conscious mind must work upon his material, but, unless that elusive something from the depths is present, his production will be no more than a design in colour, a piece of verse, or a formal tune. In other words, the skeleton and the flesh are there, but the life is absent. Similarly the person who should be enjoying the beautiful thing may simply see it as skeleton and flesh, and miss the life altogether.

To avoid misunderstanding it must be added that a proper understanding of "the skeleton and the flesh" is necessary for a full appreciation of the finished work. The viewer, reader, or listener, must have an understanding of the medium through which the "life" is presented, and education is needed in beauty as it is in truth and goodness. But this chapter is concerned more with the ultimate soul of beauty.

INSPIRATION

So far we have been thinking in general terms and trying to cover the whole field of beauty. Perhaps it will be best to select one single subject for a moment, and become more specific. Suppose we choose poetry. Most of us at some time have tried to write a poem. We choose our subject, select a suitable metre, maybe decide upon schemes of rhyme, and then express our thoughts in the most poetic words that we can find. The result is disappointing. We have produced no more than passable verse. The thing is utterly dead and uninspired.

Perhaps on another occasion we suddenly felt an idea or a phrase flooding up from somewhere into our consciousness, and knew that for a moment we had drunk from the spring of inspiration. But can we keep the spring flowing? We feverishly try to put it

within banks, to set it down so that others may drink as we have
drunk; and the result is hardly more than a ripple on the surface
of the stagnant pool of our verse. Yet at least we have sampled
something of the poet's travail. We have had a glimpse of his
inspiration, and have seen how the poet must struggle to reduce
his inspiration to a form that the world can comprehend.

Now look at the work of the poet from the opposite standpoint
—that of the reader. Unfortunately many people have had a
love of poetry killed in them, either through having to read it for
examinations, or through never having tried seriously to find anything in it. But if you have explored the land of poetry at all,
you will have found that some poetry appeals to you strongly,
while other poems leave you unmoved. What is it that moves
you? It is difficult to say. All that you know is that something
in you responds to the words of the poet, as a glass on the mantel-
piece will vibrate when a certain note is played or sung. For a
moment you have a realization of a reality that lies beyond analysis.

> Heard melodies are sweet, but those unheard
> Are sweeter; therefore, ye soft pipes, play on;
> Not to the sensual ear, but, more endeared,
> Pipe to the spirit ditties of no tone.

Keats wrote these lines in his *Ode on a Grecian Urn,* and they sum
up what poets and readers have written about poetry down the
ages.

Before trying to discover the source of life in poetry, we may for
a moment see how a similar inspiration and life enter into all art.
Several writers have collected the significant statements of artists,
poets, and musicians, in which they try to indicate how the inspiration came.

Thus the Greek poet Pindar says, "A thing said lives always a
life of longer time than any deeds, if it is something that the tongue
has fetched forth from the depths of the brain, with the good
fortune which the Graces can give" (*Nemean Odes,* IV, 9–11). This
can easily be rendered into modern psychological terms.

Keats said that he often was not aware of the beauty of some
thought or expression until after he had written it down, when it
then seemed rather the production of another person than his own.
R. L. Stevenson humorously referred to his "Brownies" who did
the main work of composing his stories for him. Mozart describes
the phenomenon of hearing the parts of some new composition not
successively but, as it were, all at once.

It would be interesting to know how far others have in a measure
had Mozart's experience. I have known several occasions when
without warning I have suddenly "seen" a sermon or a paper for
a Conference as a whole. This has always been accompanied by

a sense of compulsion to work out the "vision," as the poet or
musician has to work out the vision that he has seen.   The working
out is the labour, but it has to be done so that the life remains in
the finished product.   Let me make it clear that I am not regarding
this inspiration as prophetic, though the term "prophetic" is often
used of the poet.   But, as we shall see in Chapter XV, prophetic
inspiration is of a different order.

The Life-Energy and Inspiration

All that has been said would indicate that the element of inspiration comes from the Subconscious or Unconscious.   It follows
that the appreciation of the inspired work also depends upon the
upsurge of something from the Unconscious of the reader or
hearer, whatever part instruction and education have to play in
addition.   The work of art unlocks a gate, and lets through a
stream from a world that is as real as, or more real than, the world
of time and sense.

How can we explain it?   In Chapter I we spoke of the immanence of God.   May we visualize this immanence as constituted
by a life-force that runs through all creation?   As some sort of
analogy we have the life-principle in the body of man, which
asserts itself in different ways in each cell or member of the body.
In the universe the life-force manifests itself according to the quality
of the creature.   In the mineral world it is found as non-sentient
energy.   In the plant world it is found as unconscious life.   The
animal world has various degrees of sentiency.   In man the life-
force gives existence to a personal and self-conscious being.

One must be careful not to fall into Pantheism.   The creature
is distinct from God; and is not the unfolding of God.   God does
not depend upon the universe for His existence.   Yet the universe
remains in existence, not simply because God first created it and now
commands it to exist, but because it draws its power to exist from
the life-stream that flows through it from God.

Some people will see this easily, but others will feel that such a
theory cuts across the Biblical revelation of the separateness of God,
and of the fall of man and his need of the new birth from above.
In answer to this, we are bound, as we have seen, to give some
meaning to the doctrine of the immanence of God (p. 11).   But in
the next place we can distinguish this theory from a divine spark
in man which needs only to be fanned into a flame.   Such an idea
is contrary to the teaching of the New Testament.   Salvation is
always through the coming in of the Holy Spirit from "outside."
There is never any suggestion in Scripture that the Holy Spirit
already resides in all mankind.

The life-force which we have postulated has nothing directly to do with regeneration or new birth. It is the raw material of life that persists in a person, whether he is an unspeakable sinner or the holiest saint, whether he is a cripple or an athlete, a professor or the inmate of a mental home. Each of us has this raw stuff of life, which, if we may say so, is an impersonal energy flowing from the personal God.

We are on difficult ground here, for fear we divide the qualities of God, but any attempt to express the inexpressible is fraught with danger. Again we fall back on analogy. I am a personal being, exercising a conscious life in my daily actions. I put out my hand and lift my food to my mouth. I walk upstairs. I talk to my friends. Yet at the same time there is an impersonal aspect of my life, which controls the non-conscious bodily functions, the circulation of the blood, the digestive process, and other things. The conscious and non-conscious forms of life are not (necessarily) in conflict, nor is it inconsistent for me to have both. If a part of my body is injured or diseased, I do not necessarily use my conscious life to cut it off, but I may allow the unconscious to continue to keep it in existence, even though it has become a liability to me. Assuming that the diseased part has gone beyond the power of recovery through the unconscious life-flow, if healing comes at all it must come by a fresh intervention of my conscious life, applying the external remedy, whether ointment or knife, that alone can cure. Similarly we may believe in the presence of this impersonal life-force from God in all men without denying the need for a fresh act of God to give a new quality of life.

We may picture, then, a stream of life-energy flowing through the universe, and giving existence to all created things. It is definitely one stream, although it causes everything to exist, or live, according to its proper order. We are not conscious of its entrance into us, and so we assume that its place of entrance is in the Unconscious. If we could see inwards, and translate the invisible into visible form, we should see a stream of livingness flowing into the centre of our being from the single vast stream that flows through the whole universe. This stream is not us, nor are we the stream, but in and because of it we live and move and have our being.

Because of this life-stream we can live our day-by-day lives, building our own little world within which our Ego grows. The stream, as it were, is filtered and strained through the very con-constitution of our own personalities. But at times something fresh happens. Instead of the much-filtered water, the ego suddenly makes a more direct contact with the full stream. For a moment, maybe, the floodgates are open, only to be closed again, but in that moment we are conscious of a life that is bigger than ourselves. There is that sense of universal fitness that is the characteristic of great art. There is a realization of wholeness, since we have dipped into the river of all life.

The artist, poet, or musician, is one whose physical or mental make-up gives him frequent experiences of this stream of life at a dynamic level. He sees the soul of things, and struggles to present that soul to others. If we are receptive we also find a response arising within us as we contemplate the finished work.

This idea of inspiration does not make God the author of all poems and responsible for their sentiments. The stream of life is the raw stuff, and in making his contact with it the poet or artist has a glimpse of the soul of things. But his appreciation of what he sees is coloured by his own moral character. There is some sort of filtering even in this inspiration. Inspiration of this kind is no guarantee of moral worth. It is said that Byron wrote some of his best poems after nights of self-indulgence. Wagner, who certainly saw the soul of things, had the loosest ideas of marriage and love. Some inspired poems and works of art are definitely immoral, but their power comes because their author has built them from the raw stuff of the soul of things. Similarly a scientist can direct atomic energy to a good or evil end: it is the same power, but the use of it makes it either good or evil.

A Christian must not say that all artistic expression should be "religious" in the popular sense of the word. But it should be a revelation of the soul of things, and, where it reveals evil, it should reveal it as evil, as something to be destroyed; and never display it as a neutral thing, and certainly never with the idea of feeding evil minds under the plea of "art for art's sake."

What shall we say of much modern art on this theory? It is remarkable that literature, music and painting have in our generation produced forms of expression that many of us find discordant and impossible to understand. Where these forms are serious and not mere affectation, it is likely that the producer of them has given them to us insufficiently filtered, and has let them emerge directly from too deep a level of the mind. They have an affinity with the dreams of delirium, when the conscious mind is only half in control, or with the productions of the insane: for the mentally deranged often produce amazing pictures, meaningless to us, but significant to them, just as a dream makes sense to the dreamer but nonsense to the same person when his conscious mind is again in control. If we are prepared to accept the view of Tongues and Prophecy taken on pp. 140 ff., much modern art has an analogy with unintelligible Tongues, which cannot emerge coherently, rather than with Prophecy, which comes from the depths in an intelligible form.

CHAPTER VII

MIND, MATTER AND MIRACLES

THERE is a question and answer which go like this: "What is Mind?" "No matter!" "What is Matter?" "Never mind!"

The joke, whichever way it is interpreted, sums up what most of us feel. We have a fair idea of what we mean by "Mind" and "Matter," but why bother about how to relate these two very different things? Yet from time to time we pronounce solemnly about some happening that it shows the triumph of mind over matter.

Obviously mind, if it exists as something more than the physical brain, must have some connexion with matter, inasmuch as our own mind can direct what our material body shall do, and can, *via* the brain and nervous system, make the body do it. This is easy to accept, because we are used to it, but a moment's thought shows that we are accepting something which is very difficult to understand, and which has in fact never been explained.

An easy way out would be to dismiss the idea of an immaterial mind altogether; but most of us are reluctant to do this, and we have seen that experiments in extra-sensory perception can be accounted for only by postulating something like a mind that is over and above the physical brain.

If then this mind can affect the material part of ourselves, is it possible that it can affect matter outside of ourselves, whether inert matter or the material part of other people like ourselves? Again we begin by turning to Duke University for a modern answer. Scientific research into the problem began there in 1934 with dice-throwing experiments, and the story is recorded in Dr. J. B. Rhine's book, *The Reach of the Mind* (p. 79 f.). The subject was told to throw the dice, and to direct his mind towards obtaining either high or low numbers, or individual numbers. As with the card tests for clairvoyance and telepathy, statistics could be used to calculate whether the results of a sequence of throws were greater than the chance expectation.

Once again this was found to be so, and two new initials were added to the vocabulary of psychical research, namely P.K., standing for Psycho-Kinesis. Kinesis comes from the same Greek word as does Cinema, and means "Movement."

As soon as significant results were obtained, the test methods were tightened up to avoid any possibility of conscious or unconscious fraud, and eventually mechanical dice throwers were brought into use. Now comes a most interesting discovery, which shows that P.K. differs from a normal physical process. One can visualize a line of force going out from the mind and influencing a single die as it spins in the box or on the table, so that it turns up, say, a six. But suppose two dice are being used? Or more than two? This obviously should make it harder for the mind, just as a juggler finds it harder to juggle with many balls than with one. Yet better results were obtained when a number of dice were being thrown, as many as ninety-six being used on occasion.

The value of these laboratory tests is that they enable us to move on with greater confidence to some of the uncontrolled examples where mind is alleged to be influencing matter. We can, for instance, turn with a more unbiassed mind to the records of miracles. It has been pathetic to see even Christians, under the influence of the scientific outlook of the last seventy-five years, abandoning serious consideration of the miracles of the Bible. Modern science should lead to a very different approach. One cannot say that the experiments in P.K. have proved even one miracle in the Bible, but at least they demand that every single miracle in the Bible must be given serious consideration.

But why should we stop with the Bible? It is strange that even orthodox Christians, who will accept a miracle because it is recorded in the Bible, are chary of accepting other miracles. This is particularly true of alleged miracles that occur outside the sphere of our own denomination. The tendency has been for Evangelicals to hail any miracle within an Evangelical context as a wonderful work of God, but to regard any similar miracle, say, at Lourdes, or in a Christian Science Church, or in a Spiritualist meeting, as either a fraud, or suggestion, or the work of the Devil. Obviously, an alleged miracle might be any of these, whether it takes place in a Christian or a non-Christian context. It might also be an example of a purely neutral P.K. force, used by a good or a bad person, knowingly or unknowingly.

B. B. Warfield, in *Miracles: Yesterday and Today*, takes the line that no miracles have happened since soon after New Testament times. They were the prerogative of the Apostles and of those on whom the Apostles laid their hands. All alleged miracles since then are either spurious, or due to the influence of mind over matter, or to the "supernatural," which includes normal answers to prayer. It will be seen from this that everything depends upon the definition of *Miracle*.

WHAT IS A MIRACLE?

The reader who is interested in definitions might well pause at this point, and try to say exactly how he would define a miracle. In a first draft of this chapter the proposed definition was, "A miracle is an unusual action that cannot be accounted for by natural laws alone." The point of this definition lies both in what it omits and in what it includes. For example, it does not say "*known* natural laws"; an event is not to be classed as a miracle if it is later found to be explicable solely in terms of physical laws, as the boundaries of knowledge are extended. Again, the definition does not introduce the name of God, since there may well be other spiritual agencies, good and bad, who can be the authors of a miracle. In fact the Lord Jesus Christ Himself said that false Messiahs and false prophets would perform signs and wonders of such magnitude that even the elect people of God might wonder whether they were divine authentications of these people's claims (Matt. 24: 24). Paul speaks to the same effect in II Thess. 2: 9, 10; and in Rev. 13: 14 the evil beast, that John sees in his vision, has power to work deceptive miracles. One might add that students of the occult also make a distinction between white magic and black magic; the white magic, whether or not we regard it as miraculous, being used for beneficent purposes.

The inclusion of the word "alone" at the end of the definition covers miracles of synchronization. An event may have an explanation that is fully consistent with the observed sequence of cause and effect; yet it may be classed as a miracle. For example, the crossing of the Jordan and the fall of the walls of Jericho, recorded in Joshua 3 and 6, are likely to have come about through earthquake shocks. In 1927 an earth tremor caused a blockage of the Jordan at El Damieh, some sixteen miles upstream from Jericho, so that the flow was interrupted for nearly twenty-four hours (J. Garstang, *Joshua–Judges*, pp. 136 f., Constable, 1931). It is characteristic of earthquakes for there to be several shocks over a short period of time. If in Joshua's time one shock made the waters of Jordan "rise up in one heap, a great way off, at Adam (El Damieh?)" (Joshua 3: 16) so that the people could cross near Jericho, it is not surprising if a more severe shock threw down the walls of Jericho shortly afterwards. If this is the explanation of the events in terms of natural phenomena, the miracle lies in the fact that they occurred at the very second when God had told His people to expect them, and when, without these events, the advance of the army would have been frustrated.

This, then, was the definition originally proposed for this chapter. But discussion of it at a subsequent conference of scientists made it clear that it was far from adequate. Obviously something should be added about significance. The miracles of the Bible certainly are not spectacular conjuring tricks, but, whether they are ascribed to good or evil agencies, they have a significance in their context.

But does the Bible justify us in attempting to make a special category of events labelled miracles, and then trying to find some cast-iron definition for the term that we have used? Are we attempting to draw too tight a boundary between what we call Nature and Supernature? The Bible is a record of the mighty acts of God, and these acts appear in the realm of the natural and of the supernatural. Are we called to distinguish between them? A clear example is found in the healings recorded in the Bible, particularly the healings that are ascribed to the Lord Jesus Christ. These healings demonstrated that He was the promised Messiah, but the records of the healings do not justify us in holding that they were all performed by virtue of His Deity. Some could have been brought about through suggestion; others could have been through His use of latent powers that all men may possess in rudimentary form, and that would certainly be possessed by one who was perfect Man. We may, in fact, be acting presumptuously and foolishly if we try to fix boundaries that God Himself has not encouraged us to fix.

Yet, even if we do not attempt a definition of miracle, it would be dishonestly evasive to allow the matter to rest here. What we must face is the alleged fact that events have happened that come into head-on collision with the probabilities that science treats virtually as certainties. Without regarding this as a rigid definition, we can say that, when these events happen, those who experience them usually refer to them as miracles. It then becomes a matter for intelligent investigation whether the event is the work of an unseen spiritual being, and, if so, whether this being is God, angel, or devil. Alternatively, the event may be wholly the consequence of human agency, inasmuch as the doer makes use, consciously or unconsciously, of psychic powers that are inherent in Himself. If these powers, like ESP and PK, operate through non-physical channels, they are not altogether amenable to investigation by the physical sciences: yet it is conceivable that parapsychology may in due course become a recognized science, and be able to formulate laws that are descriptive of psychic manifestations. There is a third possibility, which is that the miraculous event is a blend of spiritual and human activity. God, or some spiritual entity, temporarily possesses a man in such a way as to direct his latent psychic powers into physical activity that appears as a miracle. If we accept some apparently miraculous phenomenon as genuine, we shall not, if we are wise, attempt to explain by which of these three ways the

effect came about. There are probably only four events that can
certainly be placed in the first category, and ascribed to the direct
action of God alone: these are the original creation of the universe,
the Incarnation, the Resurrection of Jesus Christ, and the final
acts of God at the time of the end. In saying that these four alone
can certainly be placed in the first category, we do not mean that
others may not be.

MIRACLES OF THE BIBLE

The two classes of people who find it easiest to accept the miracles
of the Bible are the simple-minded men and women of faith, and
those well-read men and women who are aware of the extraordinary
powers of the mind in certain people and in certain circumstances.
The former class may accuse the second of irreverence, and the
second may despise the former for their credulity. But it is a
common experience that what we may begin by accepting by
faith, because it is written in the Word of God, we eventually
accept as well in accord with critical investigation. Not that
critical investigation can give final proof in these cases; but it can
at least show that the belief is reasonable, and not obscurantist.
Unfortunately much theology is still bogged down with presupposi-
tions of fifty years ago, and commentators are too ready to write
off as folk stories such incidents as the floating axe-head (II Kings
6: 4–7), Balaam's ass (Num. 22: 28–30), and the three men in the
fiery furnace (Dan. 3). The man who is aware of psychic phenomena will at least consider these events as possible occurrences.
Thus there is good evidence for levitation of people and of objects
apart from anything recorded in the Bible; this is discussed later in
this chapter. A seer like Balaam evidently had the gift of clairvoyance and clairaudience (e.g. Num. 24: 4), whereby psychic
perceptions impinge upon the consciousness in the form of visions
or voices. Hence when the donkey brayed indignantly, God conveyed its meaning to the seer in the form of a human voice. There
are two other somewhat similar happenings in the Bible. One is
when the voice of God was heard from heaven in John 12: 28, 29.
Then some of the crowd heard the voice as meaningful words,
while others heard no more than the rolling of thunder. The other
occasion is when Christ spoke to Paul on the Damascus road:
from a comparison of Acts 9: 7 with 22: 9 it is clear that those
who were with him heard a sound from heaven, but only Paul
heard the sound as words. As regards the story of the fiery
furnace, there are lesser parallels in the accounts of fire-walking
and similar phenomena, which again are discussed later in this
chapter.

In all this there is no intention of explaining away the miracles, but it is right to demand that there should be a consideration of them as phenomena that are not entirely alien to other events that are known to have occurred, even if we cannot explain how they occurred.   We are probably not justified in making the distinction that some do between the so-called "Nature miracles" of the Bible, and the more personal miracles like healings, though obviously some of the nature miracles are more striking than others. The incident of the sun standing still (Joshua 10: 12–14), and the shadow going back on the sun-dial (II Kings 20: 8–11) are cases in point, although it is by no means certain exactly what occurred in the former case.   Readers of I. Velikovsky's "best seller," *Worlds in Collision* (Gollancz, 1950), will be aware of his explanation in terms of the rotation of the earth being slowed down and stopped through the close approach of a heavenly body.   His theory has not found much favour with other scientists, yet, if the motion of the sun and the moon was retarded, some explanation akin to Velikovsky's is likely.   Alternatively, a large shower of meteorites, causing dust clouds in the stratosphere, might have the effect of prolonging the daylight.   On June 30th, 1908, a large shower of meteorites, falling in Siberia, was followed by an abnormal lengthening of the daylight in Western Europe; the French papers noted it before the news of the meteorites had become known.   On the other hand several writers, who fully believe the accuracy of the Bible story, have given a different interpretation to the Hebrew account, either in terms of the sun "being silent" (as the Hebrew may mean) by going behind the clouds, and thus ceasing to scorch the pursuing Israelites, or in terms of the sun remaining bright, and not bringing too speedy a close to the day by being blotted out by the clouds.   The former is the view of the former Astronomer Royal, E. W. Maunder, set out in *The Transactions of the Victoria Institute*, Vol. LIII, 1921, and also in *The Astronomy of the Bible* (Sealey Clark, 1908); the latter is the view of Dr. A. Edersheim in *Israel under Joshua and the Judges*, p. 81–3 (R.T.S., 1877).

One could fill the book with a discussion of individual miracles. Ultimately the reason for attempting to show the credibility of the Biblical miracles is that they are to a large extent bound up with the supreme revelation of God in Christ.   The miracles of the Old Testament are part of the train of preparation for His Coming, and they form part of that Book which He Himself clearly accepted as the inspired and true Word of God.   They are not scattered in a haphazard fashion through the pages of Scripture, as one might have expected if they were purely fictitious; but they occur chiefly in two periods.   The first period is when God is bringing the people out of Egypt, and wishes to impress upon them His power and His ability to save.   In the light of the constant pull of more attractive and easy-going heathen deities, God made His presence and power felt in a way that could not be denied. Again, when He began to speak through the prophets, and when there was a determined attempt to introduce a strong rival deity, Melkart-Baal, He used Elijah and Elisha as workers of miracles. After this there is no further flood of miracles until the Coming of Jesus Christ and the launching of the Church on its mission.

TWO SUPREME MIRACLES

All other miracles sink into insignificance beside the miracles of the Incarnation and the Resurrection of Jesus Christ. The Incarnation is miraculous in itself, in that God became Man. It is impossible for us to define all that is involved in such an amazing act, but the evidence of those who knew the Lord Jesus Christ when He was on earth is set out in the Gospels, and further facts about Him are taught in the Epistles. From these one can say that in becoming perfect Man Jesus Christ did not cease to be God. The final chapter of this book attempts to draw out some of the implications of this fact.

The New Testament associates the act of Incarnation with a Virgin Birth. The evidence for such an event would be regarded as adequate, if it were not for the scientific difficulties that it raises. The only two writers who describe the birth of Jesus say that His mother was a virgin, and that the conception was through the direct act of God. These two writers, Matthew and Luke, present us with two stories that are obviously told from different standpoints, and hence represent two witnesses. Mark, who has no record of the birth, gives a probable indication that he knew of it, when he quotes the people of Nazareth as saying, "Is not this the carpenter, the son of Mary?" (Mark 6: 3). Matthew, on the other hand, having already told the story of the Virgin Birth, is free to quote others as saying, "Is not this the carpenter's son?" (Matt. 13: 55). Similarly in Paul's letter to the Galatians there is an interesting variation in the use of Greek words which suggests that he also was aware of the Virgin Birth. In Gal. 4: 23, 24, 29, he writes of the birth of Ishmael, and uses the Greek word *Gennao*, which commonly, though not exclusively, has reference to the father's act in begetting a child. In the same chapter in ver. 4 he speaks of Jesus Christ as "born of a woman," and here he uses the Greek word *Ginomai*, which is so general in scope that it is normally translated "become," and is often little stronger than the verb "to be": in this general sense it is used in Gal. 3: 14, 17, 24. Because of the scientific difficulties involved, there have been many attacks on the doctrine of the Virgin Birth, and one of the best replies to them on Biblical and textual grounds is *The Virgin Birth of Christ*, by J. Gresham Machen, (Marshall, Morgan & Scott, 1930).

Some writers have felt that the fact of parthenogenesis (Virgin birth) in certain creatures, such as bees, is helpful from the scientific standpoint when assessing the miracle of the Virgin Birth of Christ. Others have gone further.   For example, Dr. F. Sherwood Taylor, in his book, *The Fourfold Vision*, p. 47 f. (Chapman & Hall, 1945), refers to the experiment of Reimann and Miller, who caused an unfertilized human ovum to commence development by mechanical stimulation in human blood-serum containing a trace of ethyl acetate.   Another worker, G. Pincus, caused rabbit ova to begin to develop by cooling them, and then transplanted them to the uterus of another rabbit, where one female actually came to maturity. Dr. Sherwood Taylor and others have suggested that parthenogenesis may occur spontaneously on rare occasions in human beings.   If this could be shown to be true, it is most doubtful whether it would throw light on the conception of Jesus Christ, since there is yet another factor involved.   This is the question of sex determination.   The accepted view of this is that in human beings the male produces two sorts of sex chromosomes, designated as X and Y, while the ovum in the female contains the X only.   If the ovum is fertilized by an X from the male, the resultant child will be a girl; if it is fertilized by a Y chromosome, the child will be a boy.   In other words, unless a Y chromosome fertilizes the ovum, the resultant child will be a girl.   Therefore, if we were to reduce the virginal conception of Jesus Christ to a rare example of parthenogenesis, such as may occur naturally in human beings, Jesus would necessarily have been a girl.   This point is well made by Dr. E. C. Messenger in Vol. II of his book, *Two in One Flesh*, p. 90 f. (Sands, 1948).

It may be objected that this is not the whole story, since sex reversals occur among domestic fowls, and occasionally in human beings.   Readers will remember the recently publicized case of Roberta Cowell.   Yet the example of domestic fowls is not a true parallel, since in birds the female carries the sex determinant.   In human beings it may not be entirely correct to use the term "sex *reversal.*"   It would seem truer to say that there are cases of doubtful sexuality, but that ultimately there was a distinction from the beginning.   Although the basic sex distinction depends upon the XX and XY factors, the development of maleness and femaleness depends upon the functioning of organizers and secretions in the body.   It would still be true to say that such knowledge as we have of parthenogenesis only serves to intensify the need for a miracle if Jesus Christ was truly born of a virgin.   This has always been the faith of the Christian Church.   It has not been supposed that the fact of parthenogenesis made Jesus Christ divine, but Christians have felt that this manner of His coming into the world was congruent with His deity.   Scientists may be able to show that no

other man has ever been born of a virgin, but the essential thing
for a scientific statement is that it should be based upon experiments or situations where all the relevant circumstances are identical.
It may well be relevant that Jesus Christ was divine, and this fact
could lift His birth out of the category of normal births.

The bodily Resurrection of Jesus Christ must also be ranked as
a supernatural act of God, though it is just possible to maintain
that according to the natural laws of the universe a sinless man,
who suffered a violent death, would rise again on the third day.
The bodily Resurrection is more strongly attested than is the
Virgin Birth. Some modern writers deliberately play down the
evidence of the empty tomb, and think in terms of survival of
the spirit rather than of the risen body. But this is to ignore the
clear distinction that the Jews and the first Christians always made
between survival of the spirit and resurrection.

Few better books have been written on the fact of the resurrection than Frank Morison's *Who Moved the Stone* (Faber, 1930).
The book is all the more convincing in that it was apparently
planned in the first place as a refutation of the Resurrection, or at
least as a minimising of the evidence. But the examination of
the documents produced this striking book, which shows the
complete inadequacy of all attempts to account for the empty tomb
in natural terms. Friends and enemies alike admitted that the
tomb was empty. If the enemies of Jesus had removed the body,
they would have produced it, or what remained of it, when the
disciples began to preach that Jesus had risen. If the disciples
had stolen it, it would have been psychologically impossible for
them to have proclaimed so triumphantly that Jesus had risen,
risking their own lives in doing so, and to have preached a religion
of absolute truth that they knew to be based on a lie. If the New
Testament documents are treated like any other historical documents, we are left with good and solid grounds for holding that
the body of Jesus was raised from the tomb, and that He was seen
and touched on numerous occasions afterwards by His followers.
Yet the risen body was not identical in its capacities with what it
had been before death. Now it could appear and disappear, and
could pass into a room where the doors were locked. It was now
no longer subject to the spatial laws with which we are familiar.

Scientific objections to the Virgin Birth and the Resurrection
really fall to the ground. A scientist is entitled to draw conclusions
from facts that always follow when certain conditions are identical.
All conclusions about the birth and death of human beings are
deduced from men and women who are imperfect. But the evidence that we possess indicates that Jesus Christ was perfect.
Thus in Jesus Christ we have at least one unique and unrepeated
condition, which means that, as scientists, we cannot draw general

conclusions from it. We can only say that with this unique condition the historical documents indicate that certain unique results followed. If today we could repeat the conditions, and obtain different results, we should have the right to query the original evidence.

MODERN "MIRACLES" OF HEALING

If one can accept the two great miracles associated with the Lord Jesus Christ, greater probability attaches to those miraculous signs that were allegedly linked to His ministry. Many of these signs involved healing, and from the scientific standpoint so-called miracles of healing are easier to accept, since it is obvious that very similar events happen today. Even if we discount a large number on the ground that the medical evidence before and after the cure is inadequate, there remain enough cases to make us think seriously about the probability of physical disease being affected by other than material treatment. The fact is that one does not know where to draw the theoretical line in psychosomatic medicine. All that we do know is that the unity of man is such that it is commonly useless to attempt to treat the body without the mind, or the mind without the body; and a rightly adjusted mind may result in amazing healing for the body.

The field of modern "miraculous" healings is a wide one, and it is possible only to review it briefly, before attempting to draw some conclusions from the phenomena. There are, for example, certain revolutionary books by some who have the gift of healing. A typical example is *The Healing Light*, by Agnes Sanford (Arthur James, 1949). Among other cures Mrs. Sanford records the restoration of a baby who had been dead for half an hour (p. 97), and the complete recovery of a man who was dying, and whose "heart had swollen until it filled almost the whole chest . . . every valve had burst and was leaking like a sieve" (p. 101).

That body of Christians that are grouped under the general title of Pentecostalists have practised the laying on of hands for healing for many years now. There is also a quiet work going on at such places as Milton Abbas, while the Rev. F. L. Wyman has written several books, in which he speaks of cures that have come about through anointing, and through prayer circles that have been formed to pray definitely for the sick.

Roman Catholics encourage regular pilgrimages of sick people to Lourdes. Here too cures occur, but no cure is claimed as miraculous unless there is a detailed medical history of the case. The number of cures each year that are reckoned by the Roman Catholic investigators to be beyond the powers of nature to effect, amount to between five and twelve.

Many people who know nothing of the doctrines of Christian Science, respect its claims to heal. Healing services are now a feature of Spiritualism, and such mediums as Harry Edwards are reported in the spiritualist press almost every week as responsible for miraculous cures.

With this apparent wealth of evidence, one would expect to be able to find some factors common to them all, that might help in assessing the precise nature of the healings. But immediately there is a difficulty. Very few of the cures are accompanied by case histories of a type that a doctor would regard as adequate. It is extremely easy for a layman to be misled over the exact nature of a disease, and of the likelihood of a sudden turn for the better in the natural course of events. Moreover one rarely reads the sequel to the cures. Many diseases can ease up remarkably for a period, only to relapse later.

In this connexion *Psychic News* (Jan. 15, 1949) published some investigations of cures claimed by Harry Edwards, some six months previously. In Edinburgh "not all the patients had made noticeable progress, but in the majority there was improvement, with a new hopefulness and a deep sense of gratitude for benefit received." At Ilford a sufferer from disseminated sclerosis says, "It would be wrong to say I was cured by Mr. Edwards but I am definitely very much better. . . . I receive weekly healing treatment at —— Spiritualist Church, which helps me a great deal."

When one has eliminated these doubtful cases, there still remain others, both amongst spiritualists and elsewhere, that go beyond what most doctors would regard as normal. Some healers, such as F. L. Wyman, work in close co-operation with the local doctors, and one of these writes the foreword, and contributes some case notes to Mr. Wyman's books.

Assuming then that "there is something in it," is it possible to find any common factor in the different healings? Here again one finds difficulties. Some, such as Mrs. Agnes Sanford, make considerable use of the laying on of hands. She and her patients frequently feel a sensation of power flowing through her hands like an electric current. She is herself a Christian, but she does not confine her healings to Christians. Mr. Wyman commonly makes use of anointing with oil, following the injunction of James 5: 14, 15. He does not feel it right to anoint any who are not Christians, and he tries to bring them to a state of peace with God before he prays for their healing. The cures at Lourdes may occur at any time during the pilgrim's visit, but generally during some service at the Grotto there. The cures are ascribed to the intervention of the Virgin Mary.

Christian Scientists obtain their cures through the assertion of the non-reality of matter. Matter, pain, and evil, are illusions of the mortal mind, and the realization of the illusion, for oneself or for others, is the way of freedom from its supposed effects. Healing mediums generally claim to be guided by spirits, who can detect the disease and prescribe for its treatment, but Harry Edwards appears to rely on manipulations without being in a state of trance. Presumably he holds that some spirit guide is working through his touch.

Where is the common factor here? From what does the healing issue? Is it in the healer, who acts as a channel for a healing flow of divine life? Is it in the patient, in whom new forces are generated in response to faith? Or is there some healing quality in the process that is used?

The fact that some people appear to have a specific gift of healing would suggest that there is some virtue in the healer. Yet these healers cannot heal everyone. Does the healing power, then, lie in the response of faith, which is stimulated by the expectancy aroused by some well-known healer or method that has healed others? Yet even when there is a healer and a spirit of faith, there may be no healing; which would suggest that one cannot leave out of account some Power over and above that in the healer and the patient, namely God Himself. Why He should heal some and not others must remain a mystery.

The New Testament itself suggests these same sources of spiritual healing. Jesus knew that power had gone out of Him when the woman touched Him in the crowd and was healed (Mark 5: 30). In Nazareth He could do no mighty work because of the people's unbelief (Mark 6: 5, 6). And at Miletus Trophimus had to be left behind ill (II Tim. 4: 20), although Paul had the power to work miracles of various kinds, and Trophimus presumably knew this.

SOME OTHER MODERN PHENOMENA:
LEVITATION

One of the most "impossible" examples of the influence of mind over matter is the fact of levitation. Levitation is the raising of the body from the ground without any material agency, and may be accompanied by the movement of the body for some distance through the air. To the best of my knowledge this has never taken place under control conditions, *i.e.* no person who claimed to be able to levitate his body has ever allowed trained investigators to be present when he has done so.

One has to rely upon the unsupported testimony of those who claim to have witnessed levitation in the East, particularly in Tibet, or upon the testimonies of others who claim to have seen it occur during the devotions of holy men and women in the West. Two books by very different authors may be consulted in this connexion.

One is *The Physical Phenomena of Mysticism* by S. J. Thurston (Burns Oates, 1952) a Roman Catholic priest who specialized in the investigation of occult phenomena, and who is not willing to accept a "miracle" merely because it is commonly accepted by the Church of Rome. The other is *Some Human Oddities*, by E. J. Dingwall (Home & Van Thal, 1947). Dr. Dingwall was for some time the Research Officer of the Society for Psychical Research. Having met him, and heard him at question time at meetings, I know that he is not easily convinced of the genuineness of phenomena.

Yet both of these writers are convinced that there is sound historical evidence for levitation. There was, for example, Joseph of Copertino, born in 1603, who became a friar, and practised extreme asceticism. It is alleged by many people, who witnessed the phenomena themselves, that on occasions of intense devotion or rapture he rose in the air, and even flew through the air for some yards over the heads of the congregation in Church. He was visited at various times by famous people of the day, and they have testified to this miraculous levitation. Even during his last illness, when a surgeon and another doctor were cauterizing his leg, he was raised off his chair with his leg stretched out in front of him, and remained in this position for a quarter of an hour. The surgeon wrote an account of this himself.

One of the most famous of the alleged levitations of modern times is that of the medium D. D. Home. Dr. Dingwall includes him in his book, and his life may be studied in a recent biography, *Heyday of a Wizard*, by Jean Burton (Harrap, 1948). He moved in high society and such men as Trollope and Ruskin attended his séances in England, while abroad he gave sittings to Napoleon III and the Empress Eugénie. It is alleged that he was levitated on many occasions, but the most famous example was one day at Ashley Place, in London, when Home was said to have floated out at one window and returned by another. There is, however, some slight conflict between the accounts as regards the height of the room from the ground (either first or third floor), and also as regards the position of the windows, and many investigators are doubtful about the story. Houdini offered to reproduce the feat, and suggested ways in which it might be done.

Probably it is wisest to preserve an open mind on the point. Observation on some of the alleged levitations at séances should now be possible through the use of the infra-red telescope, through which objects in a dark room can be seen as clearly as in daylight, and through cameras which similarly can take photographs in apparent darkness. If levitation can be demonstrated under test conditions, as it may be, it will be yet one more example of the unexpected nature of psychic laws. It will mean that, on occasions, mind can so influence matter as to cause it to defy the fact of gravity.

What are those occasions? Seemingly, occasions when the conscious mind is dormant, and the subject is in a trance-like condition, either through an ecstasy of devotion, or as a medium.

Further facts about the levitation of objects will be discussed in the section on poltergeists (p. 97).

FIRE WALKING

Some reference must be made to the strange way in which some people have proved to be immune from burning. Dr. E. J. Dingwall in *Some Human Oddities* has a chapter on the subject, and there is also a chapter in Fr. Herbert Thurston's book, *The Physical Phenomena of Mysticism*. This extraordinary immunity is well attested, and is not confined to any single type of person. Several of those who have been canonized as saints have handled blazing coals or walked unscathed through fire. St. Francis of Paula, who died in 1507, did this from time to time, and even entered a lime-kiln soon after it had been opened instead of waiting for the normal five days for it to cool.

Daniel Home on more than twenty occasions proved his immunity from fire. He carried blazing coals round the room, without any trace of burning. Moreover he had the power to make other people similarly immune if they were not afraid. Thus Lord Lindsay testified in 1869 that "eight times I have myself held a red-hot coal in my hands without injury, when it scorched my face on raising my hand." (*Report of the Dialectical Society's Committees on Spiritualism*, 1871, p. 208). These powers were also attested from personal observation by Sir William Crookes.

A number of travellers have witnessed fire-walking among natives. One correspondent, quoted by Fr. Thurston, stresses that, when he witnessed it in Ceylon, the heat given out by the prepared bed of ashes was so great that European spectators had to move back their chairs to avoid being scorched. Frederick Kaigh, a Government doctor, in *Witchcraft and Magic of Africa* (Richard Lesley, 1947), says that as a spectator he "once thoroughly singed a silk suit, to say nothing of a pair of eyebrows, through over-curiosity. The accustomed priests stroll chanting through the fire, entirely unconcerned." He once saw a woman carry a baby through the fire (pp. 9, 10).

In all these fire-walkings there is no trace of injury on the skin or the clothes of those who have passed through the fire. The results are similar to what is recorded in Dan. 3: 27 of Daniel's three friends "the fire had no power upon their bodies, nor was the hair of their head singed, neither were their hosen changed, nor had

the smell of fire passed upon them." Although this story in the
Bible is often treated as an allegory there are reasonable grounds
for taking it seriously in the light of modern parallels. This is
not to make light of a miracle, for there is no indication that the
three friends were familiar with the "technique" of fire-walking,
and moreover their ordeal lasted considerably longer than if they
had walked several times through a trench of glowing embers.
The story indicates that they were specially equipped for the
ordeal through the presence of an angel (3: 25).

Those who had TV sets in 1937 may remember that the first
outside feature to be televised was a fire-walk in the grounds of
Alexandra Palace. The trench of burning wood embers was 12 feet
long, with a surface temperature of 800 degrees Centigrade (boiling
point for water is 100 degrees). A Muslim named Ahmed Hussain
and an undergraduate Reginald Adcock both walked the length
of the trench without injury.

CONCLUSION

The line of explanation of any apparent miracle must be sought
in the relation between Mind and Matter. If Mind can affect
Matter at all, there seem to be times when it can affect it to a supernormal degree. Laboratory experiments may be able to demonstrate PK effects to a small degree. History and experience present
examples of various degrees of significance. In speaking of Mind
we do not refer only to the human Mind. If the human mind can
operate directly upon Matter, the Mind of God can do so to an
even greater degree. It is not always necessary to postulate the
violation of any normal scientific laws. For example, in Dr.
Rhine's experiments with influencing the fall of dice, it would be
possible in theory to account by physical cause and effect for every
face of the die that came uppermost. Yet at some stage, or stages,
one is justified in assuming a non-physical control by the mind.
Similarly when Christians come together for special prayer for
fine weather or for rain, they do not look for any violation of the
laws of meteorology; but they believe that the Supreme Mind
can exercise the necessary PK effect and bring the weather that is
needed; even though the meteorologist afterwards will be able to
account in the regular way for the unexpected alteration. To some
Christians this may sound irreverent; but unless we are to visualize
God as physically moving the clouds about, this is precisely what
we do expect when we pray prayers of this type.

We must also suppose that in some men and women, if not in
all, there are latent gifts that may emerge as the mobilization of
some immaterial force that can be directed to material ends. These
gifts may be used in support of some system of belief, or without

reference to any system of belief at all. They may emerge as a power to heal, though the patient can erect a barrier to them by himself adopting a negative attitude of mind. They may be cultivated through an exacting system of training, so as to produce the astounding feats that are ascribed to certain yogis. Or they may be released suddenly, as has happened to some of the devout (and sometimes psychologically unstable) saints and mystics of the past, and to some of the spiritualistic mediums of the past and present.

In other words, miracles happen, but usually they prove nothing. Jesus Christ was aware of this when He refused to work a miracle to convince the people of His day (Mark 8: 11, 12). Yet miracles did flow out from His ministry inevitably, and the quality of the miracle, linked to the glory of the revelation that He came to give, was self-authenticating to those who had eyes to see. In particular, although He would not work a miracle as a sign, He spoke of His inevitable Resurrection as the supreme sign for His generation, and, we may add, for ours (Matt. 12: 38–40).

SUPPLEMENTARY NOTE
HEISENBERG'S PRINCIPLE OF INDETERMINACY

No mention has been made of Heisenberg's principle in this chapter, although it is often thought to be relevant to miracles. Heisenberg showed that we cannot by the nature of our methods measure simultaneously both the velocity and the position of an atomic particle. There is a fundamental indeterminacy at the basis of physics. Yet no physicist concludes that the movements of particles collectively are unpredictable. With their statistical conclusions modern physicists are in this case somewhat on a par with workers in other statistical fields. Thus an insurance company has figures that are reliable in the mass, even though it is impossible to say in advance that any specified individual will die, or have a serious accident, during the year.

If Heisenberg's principle has any relevance at all, it probably is that "the uncertainty principle has shown us that our evidence for determinism in nature is not ultimately convincing. If we cannot prove that *any* events are determined by the laws of nature (other than statistical laws), what right have we to say that science is incompatible with belief in miracle?" (Dr. R. E. D. Clark, trans. of Victoria Institute, 1952. p. 51).

CHAPTER VIII

THE TESTIMONY OF OCCULTISM

OCCULTISM is a difficult word to define, and it covers large tracts of territory. In this chapter we shall look at what some people claim to have discovered about the inner powers and inner life of man. The word "occult" means "hidden," and occultism is concerned with the hidden side of life. Some branches of psychology are also concerned with hidden things of the mind, but occultism has the hidden areas well mapped, and knows how the secret powers can be mobilized for good or evil. To step into the world of occultism for the first time is to find oneself in a bewildering existence, well signposted with eastern words, and with things taken for granted that are undreamed of by the ordinary man.

Yet when one looks for proof of these things, or even the first-hand experience of them, it is not easy to find it. Book after book is written, giving teachings and conclusions, yet the writers do not appear to have had the experience of what they record. Ultimately one may be referred back to Adepts in Tibet, and to Masters in other eastern countries, who have handed on the Ancient Wisdom, and who have penetrated the veil of sense and proved these things for themselves.

An organized form of occultism in this country is the Theosophical Society, drawing its teachings largely from eastern thought. Anthroposophy, founded by Rudolf Steiner, has some ideas in common with Theosophy, but draws more upon western traditions, and upon the intuitive awareness of Steiner. There is also much unattached occultism, with exponents of various degrees of balance and credibility, and with such semi-popular periodicals as *Prediction*. A single number of this magazine will give a fair idea of the scope of occult ideas.

Of modern writers who appear to have had first-hand experience of the things of which they write, we may mention two. Paul Brunton has travelled widely, and in his books he records how he has been accepted by eastern Masters of the Ancient Wisdom; he certainly describes strange experiences. Dr. Alexander Cannon, who has written standard books of medical and psychological science, has also written of his adventures in the occult.

THE NATURE OF MAN

From these and other writers we can gather a general view of what man is supposed to be. Basically he is a being who exists in seven bodies. We need not enumerate them all, and indeed the names differ in different writers. The term *bodies* can be misleading, for only one of the bodies is physical. It may be truer to call them *planes of existence*. Often these planes of existence are interpreted in terms of vibrations, each plane having its own "wave-length." In this life the grossest of these bodies is dominant, but at death the other six bodies withdraw, leaving the physical body to decay. The next lowest body is the Astral, and after death the man exists primarily on this plane, which is described as "the vehicle of the lower thought and desire." After continued life on this plane, he passes to the Mental Plane, the next of the bodies and so on. Eventually he retraces his steps, gathering grosser "matter" around him, until once again he is reincarnated in a physical body. The subject of reincarnation will come up again in Chapter XII.

This is the standard Theosophical view. Dr. Cannon has a slightly simpler exposition, which seems to be different from that of Theosophy. In his book *The Power Within* (Rider, 1950), he writes as follows, "Man has three co-existent, interpenetrating and conjoined vehicles of the ego, referred to in the Holy Bible as the 'three in one'." (We may note in passing that the Holy Bible nowhere uses this expression.) "The physical body is the outer manifestation of the astral or soul-body, which in turn is animated and informed by the etheric body or soul (spirit), the seat of the One Universal Life-force" (p. 22). Of the astral body he writes, "Its organs correspond to those of the physical body, when active, and when passive it looks like a large egg of yellowish hue, hence the Biblical term 'golden bowl' (Eccles. 12: 6). The 'eye' of the astral body gives the faculty of clairvoyance, and its 'ear' that of clairaudience; it is referred to in the Bible (St. Luke 11: 34) 'If thine eye be single, thy body shall be full of light.' In other words, if one develops this 'astral' vision, one becomes happy, wise and glorious. By the astral body, emotions are transmitted to the ego or self, and for this reason the astral body is often referred to as the 'emotional body'" (p. 23).

One further quotation may be made from Dr. Cannon's book, because it provides yet another example of an appeal to the Bible for support. "These facts, through all recorded time, have been known in the sanctuaries of Initiation, and formed part of the science of the soul disclosed in the mysteries of the secret temples of the East. Jesus taught these in the form of parables to his twelve disciples, calling them the 'Mysteries of the Kingdom of Heaven'" (p. 25).

Before going further, one must notice how easy it is to make a statement of this kind, and how impossible it is to prove or to disprove it. From quite early days there have been variant forms of Christianity that claimed to be based upon secret teachings of Jesus Christ, and in particular the Gnostics held views that bear a startling resemblance to those of Theosophy today.

The Christian attitude is entirely different. While we do not deny that the Bible contains deep truths that need careful interpretation, we hold that all that is essential for salvation is revealed in the pages of Scripture; that there is not the slightest indication that Jesus Christ gave a set of esoteric teachings to be handed on by word of mouth by an inner circle of initiates. The witness of the Epistles is clear, that the first disciples taught the full contents of the Gospel that had been committed to them, without a hint that there was a different Gospel for more advanced Christians.

There are perhaps two passages that could be interpreted differently. In I Cor. 2: 14—3: 3 Paul indicates that the "natural" man and the "carnal" Christian are defective in their appreciation of the things of God. The former is defective because he is lacking in the initial requirement—the possession of the Holy Spirit. The latter is defective because, in spite of his new birth, his mind is still set on the standards of this life. The other passage is Heb. 5: 11–14, where the writer speaks of his readers as babies, who continue to live on a diet of milk when they ought to have progressed to solid food.

These passages indicate that Christians may be extremely deficient in their knowledge and experience of Christian truths, but there is no suggestion that they could be initiated into knowledge and experience of an entirely different order. It is helpful to turn to the Epistles to the Ephesians, Philippians, Colossians and I John, which represent the high-water mark of Christian theology. There is nothing in these letters that is not already present in some form in the rest of the New Testament, and Colossians in particular contains strong warnings against variant forms of Christianity that appear to be of a Gnostic type. Certainly Paul finds it necessary to point out that Christian completeness is to be found in Christ, and not in some additional experience or knowledge of spiritual powers. (See e.g. Col. 2; Phil. 3).

This has been something of a digression, but it has been necessary in order to call attention to a point that will arise from time to time. The reputation of the Bible, and of the Lord Jesus Christ, who is the climax of the Biblical revelation, is so great that no claimants to a complete religion or philosophy can afford to ignore it. But the only way in which some of these strange birds can shelter in the branches of the Christian Faith is by postulating additional secret teachings of Jesus Christ, or by picking out occasional sentences and asserting that Christians do not know how to interpret their own Religion.

THE ASTRAL BODY

The astral body is a case in point. To say, as Dr. Cannon does, that it is referred to in the Bible as "the golden bowl" and the inner "eye," is a purely speculative interpretation. Others have interpreted the golden bowl of Eccles. 12: 6 as the head of man. Moreover Dr. Cannon interprets "the silver cord" in the same verse of the etheric body (p. 24), whereas other occultists refer it to the life-cord that is said to continue to bind the astral body to the physical when the astral goes "travelling." The "eye" of Luke 11: 34 can hardly represent the capacity to have clairvoyant vision, since clairvoyance is nowhere in the New Testament represented as the goal of Christian living. The verse most naturally means that singleness of attention directed to God brings light, whereas divided attention, when the mind becomes involved in a variety of aims, will bring darkness. The verse is, in a way, another version of the statement that it is impossible to serve God and mammon, and in fact in Matt. 6: 22–24 the two sayings occur together.

To return to the subject of the astral body, which is thought to be the nearest to the physical body. It is a basic belief of occultism that the initiate may consciously experience life on the astral plane even in this life, and may actually leave his physical body and travel in the astral body to different parts of the world. Here perhaps we may distinguish between actual facts and theories intended to explain the facts. It seems to me to be a proved fact that apparitions of living people have been seen by friends many miles away. It is also a proved fact that some people have become aware of events taking place many miles away, as though they had been spectators of these events. Instances will be given on pp. 116, 121. It is possible to account for these things by saying that some entity (astral body, etheric double, soul, mind, spirit) leaves the body and travels to the scene, where it either appears to someone else or witnesses some event. Or, as we have seen, it is possible to hold that the mind at a certain level has an extension in space and in time, so that a person can become aware of what is happening to another person over long distances, and build up a picture of events as they are. Or one may abandon any attempt at an explanation in terms of our present knowledge. In no case are we bound to accept the Theosophical occultist explanation if we accept the fact.

ASTRAL PROJECTION

With this in mind we may turn to the most famous modern exponent of travelling in the astral body, or Astral Projection, as it is called. Sylvan Muldoon and Hereward Carrington have collaborated in the production of three books, *The Projection of the Astral Body*, *The Case for Astral Projection*, and *The Phenomena of Astral Projection*. (The first and last of these are published by Rider, the last in 1951. I have not seen the second.) Dr. Hereward Carrington is well known as an investigator of physical phenomena, but Sylvan Muldoon is the one who has had the experience of astral projection.

According to these books, the astral body fits within the physical body, and is able to leave the physical during sleep. It has the shape and form of the person himself, and when it leaves the physical body it remains attached to it by a thin life-line, which is attached to the head, though others speak of it as attached to the solar plexus.

Muldoon believes that in sleep the astral body normally moves slightly out of adjustment with the physical, and that the purpose of this is to facilitate the recharging of the astral with cosmic life-energy. But the projection, of which he speaks in his book, is actual travelling, and Muldoon claims to be able to practise this during sleep almost at will. He is absolutely confident of this, and describes his movements and experiments in full detail. He turns and examines the life-cord, estimates its size as he moves nearer to his physical body or further away, looks at his sleeping physical body, travels to houses where he has not been before, and sees things that he later finds to be authentic.

Now it is possible to dismiss the whole thing as pure fiction, on the ground that "such things just don't happen—at any rate to me." Personally I should be reluctant to adopt this attitude immediately. It savours too much of the unscientific approach that a Christian so much deplores when the Virgin Birth and the Resurrection of Jesus Christ, and other Biblical miracles, are dismissed out of hand without further investigation. Muldoon's accounts have a certain wholeness about them that leave an impression that he is describing what he believes to be the truth. Yet what is lacking is some third-party evidence that would help to back up Muldoon's explanation of his experiences.

Perhaps we are demanding rather too much. There are occasions when someone else became aware of Muldoon's presence with her, but this could be accounted for along the lines of telepathy and clairvoyance. There are also a few occasions when in his astral body Muldoon says that he was able to move some

physical object.   Once, for example, when taken seriously ill, he
went for help in his astral body to the room where his mother and
brother were sleeping, and managed to lift their mattress and tumble
them out of bed (*The Projection of the Astral Body*, p. 200 f.).   Curiously enough, on this occasion there was a gap in his consciousness
at the moment when he was supposed to be rolling up the mattress.
On another occasion he woke himself by hammering with a wrench
on a large oil tank, and heard the blows still sounding as he woke.
Three other people testified that they heard the noise of the blows
although they could see no one near the tank (p. 202).   This evidence as stated is entirely inadequate.   Who were the three, and
did each one get up in the night and go out to look at the tank in
the dark?   The event took place some time after 3 a.m.   The
incident of the mattress also is not completely convincing.   We
are dealing with an occasion of sudden illness, the shock of being
awakened suddenly, and then a recollection afterwards of what
actually occurred.

The only other similar event that I can discover in the book is
when on two occasions Muldoon claims to have started a metronome in an adjoining room (p. 38, 39).   Certainly the metronome
started, since once Muldoon, and once his brother, had to get up
and stop it.   But one would like more evidence of the statement
that "there is no possible way in which that device can start itself."
Moreover one cannot rule out the possibility of sleep-walking.

There is, however, one curious thing about this incident and the
wrench incident.   Although Muldoon claims that his astral body
hammered on the tank, he heard the blows after he had returned
to bed.   With the metronome, Muldoon dreamt that he started
it, then awoke in his physical body, and about one second later
the metronome began to tick.   The fact that Muldoon mentions
these strange time factors proves to me, at least, that he is not
deliberately inventing his experiences.   Yet both experiences can
be explained as ordinary dreams.   There may have been someone
else hammering on the tank, and the beat of the metronome, accidentally started, may have registered upon Muldoon's mind in his
sleep, awakened him, and only then was comprehended by his
consciousness for the first time, so that the first beat consciously
registered was assumed to be the first actual beat.   Muldoon does
not say the speed at which the metronome was set.   It may have
been set to beat at approximately one-second intervals.

The most recent book, *The Phenomena of Astral Projection*, contains
the experiences of many other people besides Muldoon, some well-
authenticated, others more doubtful.   They are classified under
headings such as, *Projections produced by drugs and anæsthetics*, *Projections
at the time of accident or illness*, *Experimental and hypnotic projections*.

Several cases are given of people who saw their bodies on the operating table during the operation, and were able to reproduce afterwards the conversation of the doctors. Could not the conversation have registered on the mind even under an anæsthetic? One has heard of several cases where an unconscious person has remembered later the visit of a clergyman to the bedside and the words that he spoke. We *can* explain this by astral projection, but need we do so? In any event, such cases, like cases of appearances of the spirit at the time of death, need not be disputed by the Christian, who accepts the fact that something leaves the physical body at the time of death, and perhaps at the time of near-death.

The chapter on hypnotic projections is disappointing. Only one example involving hypnotism is given, and this may be no more than the drawing out of latent clairvoyant and telepathic faculties, under hypnotic suggestion. Dr. Alexander Cannon claims to have done the same sort of thing.

At the moment of writing I am in touch with a doctor who hopes to discover a method of photographing the astral body when it is separated from the physical. This will involve the hypnosis of a suitable subject, and the command to project the astral body in front of a special screen, where its outlines may be photographed by a film that has a greater range than a normal film, presumably at the ultra-violet end of the spectrum. But until such a picture is produced, we can only reserve judgment.

Autoscopy is the technical term for the seeing of oneself outside of oneself. It is recognized by doctors and psychologists as a rare, but genuine, phenomenon, though, strangely enough, the word does not appear in James Drever's *Dictionary of Psychology*. An article on it by Dr. Jean Lhermitte in the *British Medical Journal* of March 3, 1951, was followed by a discussion from the psychological standpoint by J. C. Flugel in the *Journal of the Society for Psychical Research* of May–June, 1951.

The problem is to account for the phenomenon in physical or mental terms. It is tied up with the explanation of how we are aware of our body-form in the first place. It is not simply that we have seen ourselves in mirrors or photographs, but we come to experience our body and its parts through the action of our nervous system. A disorder of the nervous system can distort our awareness of parts of our body. Thus we may feel that our arm or our leg does not belong to us: when a leg has been amputated, the patient from time to time feels that the leg is still there. So it may be that in a few extreme cases the nervous mechanism so breaks down that it registers the whole body as being "elsewhere," giving me, when I am sitting at my desk, the stimuli that are appropriate to myself standing by the door.

Professor Flugel in his article also introduces the idea of projection, a well-known psychological term for the reading of one's own repressed ideas, good or bad, into other people or situations. We may, for example, spend much time in fighting in other people some bad thing that we will not face in ourselves. In extreme cases the bad idea may clothe itself in the form of a vision or a voice, and it could be that the vision took the form of "my good self" or "my bad self."

It is clear from Flugel's article that much work has still to be done in the investigation of autoscopy. He does not mention any experiments under hypnosis, but this is the type of phenomenon that probably has been studied in this way. The purpose of introducing this note is to indicate ways in which explanations have been looked for other than that of the astral body. The explanations would not, however, fit the "astral projection" of Muldoon and others, if the facts are as these travellers state them to be.

The Aura

Before leaving this subject, we must say something about the possible existence of an aura, though, if it exists, there is probably nothing occult about it. Many people with gifts of clairvoyance claim to be able to see an aura around the human body, and to be able to tell facts about the health, vitality and disposition of a person from the colour and apparent composition of this aura.

Shortly before the first World War the study of the aura was put upon a scientific basis for any who have cared to follow it up. The pioneer was Dr. W. J. Kilner, of St. Thomas's Hospital, London. He worked on the assumption that the alleged aura might be an emanation of the ultra-violet range of light. He therefore constructed a viewing-glass, containing a dye that would exclude certain light rays and make the viewing of ultra-violet more feasible. The dye that he used was an alcoholic solution of Dicyanin.

In his book *Human Atmosphere* (Routledge, 1920), he describes his method. The observer looks through the glass at a fairly bright light for a minute or two, and then looks at a person standing against a dark background in a dimly-lighted room. With practice it should become possible to observe a faint mist around the person, following roughly the outlines of the body, and extending some inches out from it. Dr. Kilner certainly observed this.

A later writer, Oscar Bagnall, made similar experiments, and has recorded them in *The Origin and Properties of the Human Aura* (Kegan Paul, 1937) and more recently in articles in *Country Life* (June 23, 1952, April 12, 1951). It is difficult to discover just what effect the dicyanin screen, as it is called, has upon the eyes, though it has a temporary effect of correcting long sight. Both Kilner and

Bagnall tested the focus of their eyes with a microscope, setting
the focus accurately before looking through the screen, and finding
that they needed to refocus after their eyes had been sensitized.

Bagnall does not suppose that there is anything mystical about
the aura, nor does he connect it with any astral body.   But he finds
that ill-health and diseases of certain organs are reflected in the condition of the aura.   "Diseased organs emit a very faint aura, if
any" (p. 32).   One might be tempted to connect the aura in some
way with the electrical currents that are generated by all living
tissue, and that can be recorded by such an instrument as the
electroencephalogram or toposcope, which reveal the electrical
activity in the brain.   The frequencies, however, are not of the
order that could be visible to sight, any more than frequencies
used in radio and TV can become visible without being translated
by a machine.   We can fall back on the vague idea of radiation
from a living body of a type that is just beyond the borderline of
normal vision.   Or we can use even vaguer terms, and speak of
"a higher octave of energy waves, but . . . certainly something
different from the range covered by phenomena known in the
physical world."   The latter is the description by the clairvoyant,
Phoebe Payne, in *This World and That*, p. 102 (Faber, 1950).

Some people claim that the auras of two individuals who dislike
one another, flash and spark in opposition when they come into
proximity; hence the instinctive dislike of two people for each
other on apparently irrational grounds.   But Bagnall finds no
evidence for this.   Incidentally, a dead body is said not to emit
an aura of any kind.

CONCLUSION

In this chapter we have been able only to touch the fringe of
occultism, and have selected a few of the views about the nature
of man, and quoted examples of astral projection which might
possibly be held to prove the existence of something like a soul,
having the same shape as the physical body.   The whole philosophy
of occultism goes far beyond the scope of this present book, though
a later chapter will discuss the teaching of reincarnation, which
forms a basic part of most occult philosophy.   Although occultism
frequently clashes with the Biblical revelation, which Christianity
accepts, many of the "discoveries" of occultism may well be valid.
The Christian accepts that there are psychic forces that may be
unleashed by those who understand the technique.   The thing
that is uncertain is the legitimacy of unleashing these forces deliberately, and also the danger of building a doctrine of God and man
upon these psychic experiences.

CHAPTER IX

THE EVIDENCE OF SPIRITUALISM

A SHORT time ago I was speaking on the subject of Christianity and Spiritualism. The chairman in his opening remarks expressed the hope that I would tell the meeting the difference between Spiritualism and Spiritism. The answer is that "Spiritism" is a kind of nickname given to the Spiritualist Movement by its opponents. Personally, I avoid using it, partly out of courtesy, and partly because by using it I should imply that all the Spiritualist manifestations are due to spirit agency, and I do not believe that they are. It may equally be argued that Spiritualism is not specially spiritual, and this is true: but at least the title is the commonly accepted one, and as such I propose to use it.

It is estimated that there are some 50,000 members of Spiritualist churches and groups in Great Britain. The largest group is the Spiritualists' National Union, which now incorporates the Lyceums, which cater particularly for children and young people. Another group is the Greater World Christian Spiritualist League, which carries on much healing and philanthropic work. Two other major bodies are the Marylebone Spiritualist Association, and the London Spiritualist Alliance, of which the latter is more of an investigation society than are any of the others, and its interests are reflected in its monthly magazine, *Light*, which is probably the most open-minded and the most highbrow of the Spiritualist journals. There are also a group of White Eagle Lodges.

The reason for the existence of these different organized bodies is twofold. First, people commonly desire some kind of credal belief, and the founders of these organizations naturally incorporated into them either their own beliefs, or those that came through the mediums. Secondly, Spiritualism lends itself so easily to fraud, that these reputable organizations, for their own protection, do their best to sponsor only reliable mediums.

It will be noticed that I have not included the Society for Psychical Research in the list of Spiritualist organizations. This Society, founded in 1882, is not a Spiritualist body, but exists for the serious scientific investigation of all the phenomena that can be classified under the heading Parapsychology. Its careful investigations and high standards have gained it a reputable name. Some of its members are Spiritualists, some are not.

THE MANIFESTATIONS OF SPIRITUALISM

Spiritualism claims a number of varied manifestations. Most of the phenomena take place in darkness. This naturally arouses suspicion, but we know so little about the laws that govern the phenomena, that we cannot insist that they should take place in broad daylight before we will believe them. After all, the development of a photographic film commonly needs a dark-room.

Primarily, we shall consider Spiritualism as the alleged communication with the spirits of the departed. This may take several forms, of which the following are representative:

1. The "spirit" moves some object, such as a little board on wheels, or a tumbler, upon which the sitters' hands are placed. The board moves so as to write a message, or so as to spell out answers by going from letter to letter on an alphabet on the table. With this method it is extremely difficult to avoid an unconscious guiding of the board.

2. A medium (man or woman) communicates information from the departed to members of the audience or the circle. In a hall or public service the medium will normally be in full view of the audience, and in the normal lighting of the hall. In his own voice he passes on messages to individuals, sometimes pointing to them, sometimes appealing for anyone who recognizes a name or description to answer. Generally points of identification are given to indicate who the message is from on the other side. Some family joke, or other incident, is alluded to. The majority of the messages are accepted by the recipients as accurate, and advice given is frequently found to be relevant. Spiritualists refer to this form of communication as clairvoyance, which it may well be. There seems no need to postulate spirit intervention. The communication of one mind with another, transcending sense and time, is sufficiently well authenticated, as we have seen. The fact that the medium ascribes the information to the spirits does not prove that this is the real source of it. The facts as they pass from one mind to another (if we may use spatial terms without being taken literally) are projected as voices or visions into the consciousness of the medium.

3. The medium goes into a trance, and his or her body appears to be possessed by a control spirit, who passes the information from other spirits to the sitter, or inquirer. It is common for a medium to have one main control repeatedly, or not more than three or four. Thus, as we have seen, Miss Winifred Moyes is controlled by Zodiac. Several controls profess to be Red Indian Chiefs who died centuries ago. The control speaks in quite a different voice from that which the medium normally uses. It is,

in fact, as though the personality of the medium had been suddenly switched to another personality.   The control is, in fact, *in control*.

4. A further step is "direct voice" mediumship.   Here there is commonly a control, but this control has a similar function to the announcer in such a programme as "In Town Tonight." The only private séance that I have attended was of this kind, and this is exactly the impression that I received.   I went because I was trying to investigate the claims of Spiritualism, and a Minister of another denomination asked me to go with other Ministers in the hope that some worthwhile message would come through. This is evidently the third séance that Dr. Leslie Weatherhead refers to on p. 106 of his *Psychology, Religion and Healing*.   I am not so convinced of the genuineness of this particular séance as he seems to be, in view of the fact that two of the "spirits" who spoke could not, or would not, answer a simple question, one about the name that her friends had called her when she was on earth, and the other about the name which he used to call the sitter whom he was now addressing.   But, genuine or not on this occasion, it was a direct voice séance, and it was uncanny to hear the different voices, educated and uneducated, a man, two women, and a boy, coming, so far as could be judged in the dark, from slightly to the side of the medium.   This medium did not go into a trance, and was able to speak in his own voice provided that the spirits were not speaking.   I was told that he had been observed through an infra-red telescope, by which it is possible to see in a room which is pitch dark to normal vision, and that his own mouth was not moving while the other voices were speaking.

Sometimes the spirits are supposed to speak through trumpets which are placed beyond the reach of the medium, and which often float in the air.   Their purpose is to magnify the voice and make it audible.

5. Besides these communications, there are the physical phe-nomena of the séance-room.   These are admittedly extraordinarily difficult to assess.   In many ways, the most suitable investigators are conjurors, and from time to time those members of the Magic Circle, who specialize in such investigations, put on fictitious séances.   One such "séance" was given for members of the Press, and was photographed and reported in *Everybody's* of October 9, 1948.   Members of the séance who were not in the secret were loud in their praises of the phenomena and of the messages.   Prob-ably the most notorious case of fraud in recent years were the "materializations" produced by Mrs. Helen Duncan, who was ultimately convicted in court.   Photographs of some of her materialized figures show them to be made of cheese-cloth.   It does not, however, follow that none of her manifestations were genuine.   Most physical mediums who have submitted to tests

have been detected in fraud from time to time, even when at other times their results have almost certainly been genuine.

It must be sufficient to mention here the two brothers, Willi and Rudi Schneider, who were tested by practical investigators under the most rigid conditions, not only in their own home, but in test laboratories. The story of Rudi Schneider was written by Harry Price (Methuen, 1930). Under these test conditions luminous objects were moved about the room, a toy zither played by itself, heavy tables were raised from the ground, a musical box played and wound itself up again, and objects resembling legs and arms were pushed out from a curtained cabinet several feet from where the medium was held. At times, to eliminate any chance of collusion, each sitter was under an electrical control, so that if one hand or foot was moved a red light would flash on.

MATERIALIZATIONS

The mention of the objects like legs and arms brings us to another piece of physical mediumship, namely materializations. A whitish substance, known as ectoplasm, exudes from the medium's body, and grows into shapes and figures. This substance cannot endure more than the dimmest light. Sudden light will cause it to disintegrate or to leap back into the medium's body. It is not easy to substantiate apparently authentic claims that ectoplasmic figures have been photographed, and, more remarkable still, have dipped their hands and wrists into melted paraffin wax, leaving wax "gloves" behind them when they dematerialized, the wrists of the gloves being too narrow for a solid hand to have been withdrawn without breaking them. There are some salutary lessons in deception and self-deception in this field to be learned from D. J. West's book, *Psychical Research Today*, p. 59f. (Pelican).

Suppose we grant that the evidence is adequate for materializations and other physical phenomena: have these manifestations proved the fact of survival? Certainly the ordinary physical phenomena need have no connexion at all with departed spirits. The throwing about of furniture and playing of zithers is no indication of the presence of your deceased grandfather, unless he used to do that sort of thing when he was on earth! It is possible that some spirit moulds the ectoplasm that comes from the medium. But in view of the experiments of Dr. Rhine and others in Psychokinesis, I should myself not dismiss the possibility that the moulding of the ectoplasm is due to the medium's own mind. Similarly the moving of objects may also be an intensified P.K. effect. Obviously, to name it P.K. explains nothing; but if lesser P.K. operates without the aid of spirits, there is no reason why it should not operate in an intensified form as an extension of the powers of mind.

In this list of Spiritualistic effects I have not included healings, tongues, prophecy, psychometry, or angels. Healing forms a regular part of Spiritualism, and such healers as Harry Edwards obtain the most remarkable results. In the chapter on *Mind and Matter* I have already discussed such healings. They do not appear to be relevant to a discussion of Spiritualism as such. Psychometry has also been considered (p. 46) and in fact some Spiritualists do not regard it as having any evidential value. Tongues and prophecy will be noticed later (pp. 140 ff.) Angels are not the exclusive prerogative of Spiritualists: they are not spirits who have lived on this earth. Again, we shall consider them in the next chapter.

COMMUNICATIONS WITH THE DEPARTED

In estimating Spiritualism we ought to centre on the fundamental claim of the Movement, which is communication with the spirits of the departed. When some years ago a group of Spiritualists asked me for a public debate on "The Bible and Spiritualism," we did not really get to grips with each other. I debated the attitude of the Bible towards attempted communication with the departed, while the other speaker took the line that, because Spiritualism could produce similar miracles and phenomena to things recorded in the Bible, Spiritualism was the true successor of New Testament Christianity.

If for a moment we consider what the Bible says about attempting to communicate with the departed, we may be astounded to find that, whenever this is mentioned, it is condemned as something evil. We do not refer to witchcraft. Spiritualists are as much against witchcraft as anyone, for witchcraft is the deliberate attempt to use black magic by means of evil spirit agency.

But the following passages may be noted: In Lev. 20: 6, 27, and Deut. 18: 10, 11, there are references to those who have, or who consult, "a familiar spirit" (Hebrew OB). This clearly refers to a medium with a "control" spirit, as is obvious from I Sam. 28: 7, where the phrase is used of the medium (not witch) of Endor. The passages also include "wizards" (*lit.*: "Knowing ones"), and "necromancers" (*lit.*: "Seekers of the dead," or "Inquirers of the departed").

In the Historical Books there is the incident of Saul and the medium in I Sam. 28. There are legitimate differences of opinion as to whether this séance followed the normal pattern. Certainly it would be unusual for the medium to produce a materialization without being in a trance. But, however that may be, the verdict

of the Bible on Saul's action is given in I Chron. 10: 13, where one
of the reasons for Saul's death is said to have been "because of the
word of the Lord, which he kept not; and also because he asked
counsel of one who had a familiar spirit, to inquire thereby, and
inquired not of the Lord." Spiritualists evade this verdict by
calling it "the *priestly* chronicler's homily," and saying that "Saul
did inquire of the Lord" (G. Maurice Elliott, *Spiritualism in the
Old Testament*, p. 138, Psychic Press, 1938). Obviously the Chronicler knew I Sam. 28, 6, which said that "when Saul inquired of
the Lord, the Lord answered him not neither by dreams, nor by
Urim, nor by prophets." But what he says, in the idiom of his
day, is that Saul was not content to accept the Lord's silence (which
was due to his previous disobedience), but proceeded to use forbidden means of inquiry. A similar use of an absolute negative
is found in Deut. 5: 3, where Moses says, forty years after the
covenant on Sinai, "The Lord made not this covenant with our
fathers, but with us, even us who are all of us alive this day."
Obviously he means that the Covenant was made with the fathers,
but not only with them. In view of the attitude taken up elsewhere
by the compilers of the earlier historical Books there is little doubt
that they would have agreed with the Chronicler's verdict (*cf.* II
Kings 21: 6).

There is a similar verdict in the prophets. Thus Isa. 8: 19, 20
has the following: "When they shall say to you, Seek unto them
who have familiar spirits and unto the wizards that chirp and
mutter: should not a people seek unto their God? On behalf of
the living should they seek unto the dead? To the law and to
the testimony! If they speak not according to this word, surely
there is no morning for them." There are several possible variants
in translation here: in particular it is uncertain where the quotation,
that begins "Seek unto," ends, whether at the word "mutter," or
(translating "God" as "gods") at "unto the dead." But no
alternative translation affects the prophet's bitter condemnation of
spiritualistic practices. He goes so far as to say that the truth of
what the spirits say must be tested by the revelation that God had
already given—a most important principle.

It may be argued that the Old Testament regulations have now
been set aside, and what was forbidden then, because of certain
dangerous consequences that can follow from dabbling in Spiritualism, is legitimate for us. Yet there is no indication in the New
Testament that this is so. Yet some would interpret the New
Testament as though the early Church were practising Spiritualists.
It is significant to note the absolute silence of the New Testament
in places where a believer in Spiritualism could not under any
circumstances have been silent.

In I Thess. 4: 13–18 Paul discusses the problem of those Christians who had died.   He urges those who are left behind not to sorrow like those who have no hope.   Here a Spiritualist would have added, "Come to the Service on Sunday, and comfort yourselves by speaking to them."   Instead of that, Paul urges them to wait patiently until the reunion at the Second Coming of the Lord.

Again, in I Cor. 15: 18 Paul employs an argument that he could not have used if he had been a Spiritualist.   He argues thus: If Christ has not risen from the dead, your departed relatives have perished.   But Christ has been raised: therefore they have not perished and we shall not perish.   But a Spiritualist would have short-circuited this argument, by saying, "we know our relatives have not perished, since they speak to us at our séances."

Against the weight of this silence, an attempt to use the Transfiguration as a séance is beside the point.   Such an event happened once only, the disciples were not told to repeat it, and, significantly enough, the voice from heaven on this occasion said, "This is my beloved Son, hear ye him."   The Christian similarly is not to aim at gathering information from the departed, but at hearing the message of Christ.

We note also commands in the Epistles to test the spirits (I John 4: 1, and I Cor. 12: 3).   Spiritualists often quote this command, recognizing, as they do, that there are evil spirits who try to gain control of mediums.   But in the New Testament, as well as in the Old, the choice is not between an evil spirit and a good spirit— one out of many—but a choice between the one Holy Spirit inspiring a prophet and an evil spirit inspiring him.

POSSIBLE SELF-DECEPTION

It is clear that the Biblical verdict on Spiritualism is completely hostile.   One may assume that the reason is because of the deception (conscious or unconscious) that is inherent in it.   There may, in fact, be two sources of deception.

1.   *The unconscious mind of the medium.*   We will not labour this point *ad nauseam*, but evidence goes to show that the range of the mind in time and space is so incredible, according to commonsense standards, that one hesitates to set bounds to it.   We recall Osty's experiments with Psychometrists, some of them non-Spiritualists (p. 59 f.).   Once the link, whatever it is, is established between the medium's mind and yours, you become virtually a psychometric object, and a switchboard for the past, present, and future lives of your friends.   This is equally true of proxy sittings, which are commonly thought to be more evidential than ordinary sittings, since the sitter consults the medium on behalf of someone else whose identity is not disclosed.

The testimony of Mrs. Eileen Garrett is of great interest.   Mrs.

Garrett has had the faculty of clairvoyance since she was a child, and has practised as a medium. Unlike most mediums she has spent much time in trying to discover the nature of her experiences. In one of her books, *My Life as a Search for the Meaning of Mediumship*, she has written, "In examining my own process of clairvoyance, I have become aware that I draw the knowledge which helps me build the images of the dead relatives and friends of those who need help, from the subconscious minds of the sitters" (p. 168). And again, "I began to wonder whether the whole structure of mediumship might not depend on a form of telepathy, and whether the medium does not draw information for communications from the subconscious mind of the sitter" (p. 185). It is interesting to find a recent comment by Mrs. Garrett in *Light* (April 1954): "I am often asked how I regard the controls after these many years. Recent experiments would suggest that they are external. . . . But if the day should come that I should after all find them to be figments of my subconscious, my placidity would not be again disturbed. The search for eternity continues, but the ways and means by which knowledge reveals itself no longer bewilder me."

There have been cases where the medium has received messages and descriptions from some friend of the sitter, believed to be dead, and later found to be alive. The most famous instance is the Gordon Davis case reported by Dr. S. G. Soal in the *Proceedings of the S.P.R.*, Vol. XXXV. This gives strong support for the idea that telepathy and clairvoyance play a much stronger part in séances than is often realized. Such deceptions may be regarded as fairly harmless, but they are none the less deceptions. The sitter cannot be certain of being in touch with the one who has passed on, for the medium may in fact be interpreting a projected image from the sitter's own mind.

2. A more dangerous deception would arise if we suppose *the intervention of evil spirits*. Spiritualists themselves recognize this possibility, and in one single issue of *Psychic News* there were three warnings about it. Roman Catholics, for whom Spiritualism is banned, ascribe many of the manifestations to evil spirits. This is also one regular Evangelical interpretation. It is set out strongly in a remarkable book by G. H. Pember entitled *Earth's Earliest Ages*. This book was published in 1884, but a reprint, with some small additional matter, was issued more recently by G. H. Lang (Wimborne, Dorset). It is one of the few Evangelical books to tackle the subject seriously, though with it one must couple another knowledgeable book, *Modern Spiritism*, by Dr. A. T. Schofield, who was one of the pioneers in the field of the unconscious mind, and who was a devout Christian. Both of these books are pioneer books, in the sense that the authors are not simply passing on what

others have written. Both are convinced that in Spiritualism we
are encountering demonic powers, though Dr. Schofield readily
admits other forces such as telepathy. If such evil spirits exist
—and we shall consider this in the next chapter—the indication
in Scripture is that they try to deceive, and even to possess, human
beings who open the door to them. The essence of deception is
to speak 90 per cent truth and 10 per cent error. If I were a
demon, trying to deceive a decent-minded person, I should employ
the tactics of "Lord Haw-Haw" in the Second World War. By
speaking a great amount of truth, I should hope to receive acceptance of vital errors. Thus I should propagate good advice and
philanthropy, but omit those unique pillars upon which the Christian
faith stands, the Deity and the Atoning Death of the Lord Jesus
Christ, and salvation through faith in Him.

Now the remarkable thing is, that when the "spirits" speak of
these things they almost always deny them. One can check this
in a number of Spiritualist works, but one of the most fervent
modern propagandists for Spiritualism, Lord Dowding, makes no
secret of it at the end of his book, *Many Mansions* (Rider, 1943).
He is speaking with approval of the messages received by the
medium, Stainton Moses, through the control spirit, Imperator:
"The first thing which the orthodox Christian has to face is that
the doctrine of the Trinity seems to have no adherents in advanced
circles of the spirit world. The Divinity of Christ as a co-equal
partner with the Father is universally denied. Jesus Christ was
indeed the Son of God, as also are we sons of God. . . . We
(*i.e.* Christians) are taught to believe in the Remission of Sins to
the penitent, through the virtue of Christ's sacrifice and atonement. This doctrine Imperator vigorously combats in a score of
passages throughout the book". The reader will note that these
are the teachings "in advanced circles." They are not the ideas
of those who have recently passed over.

Naturally some will say that if the teachings disagree with the
Bible, so much the worse for the Bible! Yet we would at least
plead that this difference should be recognized. In spite of the
sincerity and good faith of the Greater World Christian Spiritualist
League, we must realize that the messages of the spirits do not agree
with the Biblical revelation. If the League says that the messages
that come to them do agree—and obviously they do not agree
over the atonement at least—Lord Dowding's spirits speak in
different terms. In fact the spirit messages disagree to an absurd
extent. A leading article in *Psychic News* for May 15, 1948 truly
says, "How can we give the same message when half of us accept
reincarnation and the other half hotly deny its possibility; when
we have Christian Spiritualists, Jewish Spiritualists, Buddhist
Spiritualists, and even, according to Mr. Butler himself, Atheist

Spiritualists." I know that the retort will be, What about the Christian denominations? But our divisions are not as fundamentally extreme as those suggested in this leading article, nor do we claim to have direct communications from the unseen world to guide us in these points of interpretation over which we differ. But spiritualists claim to be in contact with spirits who can find out the truth from advanced spheres: yet a direct question about, say, reincarnation will produce one answer from one high spirit and a contradictory answer from another.

One person is impressed by evidence that leaves another person unmoved. The two pieces of evidence for genuine communication that have impressed me are the "Patience Worth" stories, and the Cross-Correspondences. The former are a series of historical novels that were received in automatic writing by a Mrs. Curran, an American woman of slight education, from 1913 onwards. Each is written in a different type of dialect. The language of *Telka*, a story of the Middle Ages, has 90 per cent of its words Anglo-Saxon, and contains no word which first came into use after the seventeenth century. *The Sorry Tale*, a story of the time of Christ (admittedly fiction) is accurate in what it says about the people and situations in the Roman Empire at that time. Such knowledge was far beyond that possessed by Mrs. Curran, and the speed at which the automatic writing came, as well as her circumstances, made consultation of libraries and dictionaries impossible.

The communicator claimed to be Patience Worth, a Dorsetshire country girl of the seventeenth century, yet, if we grant this, we are still at a loss to know how a girl of this type could obtain all the facts that she uses. Even the language in *Telka*, while not containing any word later than the seventeenth century, is said to be more of the time of Wycliffe. If it is impossible to ascribe the books to the mind of Mrs. Curran, it is not really much easier, if we think it out, to ascribe them to another country girl, even if she did live three centuries earlier. If the discarnate mind of Patience Worth gathered everything by a process of inspiration, we may at least suggest that the incarnate mind of Mrs. Curran might do the same. Inspiration is still very much of an unknown quantity. Could there be a kind of psychic reservoir of accumulated facts and knowledge which is tapped, to a greater or lesser extent, by seekers after truth, or even at times accidentally? This is not exactly what Jung means by the Collective Unconscious, nor is it quite what the Occultist means by the Akashic world record. But it might be a fact.

The other striking piece of evidence is that of Cross-Correspondences. Unfortunately, this is too technical to be summarized, but it may be studied in a book by H. F. Saltmarsh, *Evidence of*

Personal Survival from Cross-Correspondences (G. Bell, 1938). Briefly
it is alleged that a group of classical scholars, who had passed over,
determined to give proof of their survival by communicating a
number of apparently meaningless classical allusions to several
automatists, who were unaware of what was happening. When the
scripts were brought together, they would be found to throw light
on one another, and thus lead to a sensible meaning. The evidence
indicates that this happened in several cases, and the references
were obscure enough to satisfy most sceptics. It seems that we
must either accept the communications at their face value, or else
suppose that the responsible agent was the unconscious mind of
Mrs. Verrall, one of the automatists, and the widow of one of the
alleged communicators. This involves again the subconscious
switchboard idea, Mrs. Verrall being linked to the other automatists because they were engaged in the same plan, and to the
mental contents of the minds of the "communicators" as they
had existed on earth. This may sound very involved, as indeed it
is. But one fact is worth remembering. One of the alleged
communicators was F. W. H. Myers: he could apparently remember
obscure lines and allusions from the classics. Yet he could not
give the contents of a sealed letter that he had left behind at his
death to furnish a proof of his identity. It is not simply prejudice
that makes me hesitate even about the cross-correspondences.

   Psychic News carries the slogan "Life after death proved." Has
this claim been substantiated by Spiritualism? And, if it has, is this
all that we need to know—that after death man continues to exist?
Man's greatest need is to come into right relationship with God.
Merely to move him on to another existence does not meet this need.
Nor is it enough to demonstrate that he survives death: there might
well be a persistence of a mental system which would gradually
fade into nothingness. God in the Gospel promises more than
this. Eternal Life in the Risen Christ is something that begins
now, and is infinitely more than mere survival. If the Bible is
correct, to depart, for the Christian, is to be "with Christ" (Phil. 1:
23) in a manner that is closer than anything that we can know on
earth.

CHAPTER X

GHOSTS AND POLTERGEISTS

To the best of my knowledge I have only once seen a ghost. It was on New Year's Day twenty years ago, when I was taking a Service of Holy Communion at a Church to which I did not often go. In the early part of the Church of England Service the minister faces the congregation and reads, or recites, the Ten Commandments. While I was doing this, I noticed a latecomer entering by a door on my right at the back of the Church. He was an elderly man wearing a brown overcoat. Naturally his movement caught my eye, and I noticed that he moved across in front of the verger, who was at the very back of the church, and went into a pew on my left, also near the back. It was a week-day, and the congregation was small. When the people came forward at the actual Communion, as they do in the Church of England, I was surprised to find that they were all women, apart from the verger in his black gown. There was no sign of the man. So afterwards I asked the verger what had happened to the man who came in while I was reading the Commandments. He seemed surprised, and told me that no one had come in late. I persisted that he had come in by the door on my right, and had passed right in front of the verger. His reply gave me the traditional creepy feeling down the back; for he said, "He couldn't have come in by that door, sir. We always keep that door locked, except for funerals!"

So that was my ghost. Whether it was the ghost of a living or a dead person, I cannot say. Personally I think it was probably the ghost of a living man who very much wanted to come to the service on that day.

GHOSTS OF THE LIVING AND OF THE DEAD

The idea of ghosts of the living may sound somewhat surprising. But in proportion they are not uncommon according to the result of two questionnaires sent out, as far as possible at random, in 1890 and in 1948. The primary question was virtually the same in both years. "Have you ever, when believing yourself to be completely awake, had a vivid impression of seeing, or being touched by, a living being or inanimate object, or of hearing a voice; which impression, so far as you could discover, was not due to any external physical cause?" In 1890 9.9 per cent answered yes, and in 1948 14.3 per cent gave a similar answer. Further questions to these people tried to discover whether the "ghost" was that of (a) a living person, (b) a dead person, (c) an unidentified person. The percentages were as follows: (a) Living person 32 per cent (1890), 40.5 per cent (1948). (b) Dead person 14.3 per cent (1890), 9 per cent (1948). (c) Unidentified 33.2 per cent (1890), 27.5 per cent (1948). The balance of the percentages is made up by non-human apparitions. Considering the popular idea of a ghost as being someone who has died, it is surely a mark of the good faith of the answerers that ghosts of the living outnumber ghosts of the dead. (*Proceedings of the S.P.R.*, Vol. X, and *Journal of the S.P.R.*, Vol. XXXIV, No. 644–645).

To make clear what is meant by a ghost of the living, here is a well-attested case from *Phantasms of the Living* by Gurney, Myers, and Podmore (Abridged edition, Kegan Paul, 1918) pp. 156–8. A maid of Lady Waldegrave, named Helen Alexander, was taken seriously ill while she and her employers were staying at Torpoint. Another maid in the house was looking after her on the night when she died. As she was about to give the patient her medicine, she heard the door open, and saw an old lady enter, carrying a brass candlestick, and wearing a red shawl and a flannel petticoat with a hole in the front. The old woman looked at her sternly, but the maid gave the medicine to the patient. When she turned round again, the old woman had vanished. The maid had the impression that she was the mother of the patient. In the morning, after Helen had died, the maid described the vision to her employers, who later corroborated this. In due course Helen's relatives came to the funeral, and the maid recognized the mother as the apparition whom she had seen. On further inquiry she was told by another of the daughters that the clothes corresponded to what the mother would wear if she was roused in the night, that there was a candle-stick similar to the one that the apparition had carried, and that there was a hole in the mother's petticoat where the maid had seen it.

This, then, is a typical example of a living ghost. We need not at present have an illustration of a "dead" ghost. Our con-cern is how to account for the appearance of a ghost at all. It is not sufficient to say that an earth-bound spirit returns to the scene of a crime; for how would this fit in with the ghost of someone still alive? Nor is it enough to say that a person (dead or alive) telepathises a picture of himself to a friend or to some locality, for often the ghost adapts itself to the room in which the percipient is, entering by the door, avoiding furniture and obstacles, even though the room is quite unknown to the original person.

The most serious attempt to grapple with the problem is the 7th Myers Memorial Lecture (1942) by G. N. M. Tyrrell. For some time this has been out of print, but fortunately it was re-published in 1953 by Gerald Duckworth. Its title is simply *Apparitions*. A bare summary cannot do justice to the evidence and conclusions of the book, but briefly, Tyrrell employs some of the newly-established facts of the deeper levels of the mind to account for ghosts.

A ghost, according to his theory, is the result of a link-up at a deep level of the minds of two or more people. Let us suppose that A thinks strongly of B, or wishes that B knew something that was happening to him at that moment. At a certain level of the two minds, what Tyrrell calls the "Producer" and the "Stage Carpenter" get to work to enact a suitable drama that will stimulate the receiving end of B's sense perceptions, so that he will appear to himself to see, hear, or feel, a hallucination of A. The picture will be given the suitable clothes, or even such material accom-paniments as carriages and horses. If other people are present, the deep level of their minds may also be drawn into the drama, and they too will experience the hallucination, perceiving the non-material ghost as though it were occupying physical space, whereas, when the ghost has gone, no trace of its presence will be left on the surroundings.

Tyrrell's explanation does justice to the facts, and, if it is accepted, it means that dead persons who appear have survived death, and their minds initiate the drama of their appearance, just as do the minds of living "ghosts." The alternative is to introduce the idea of delayed telepathy. We have seen how the mind has a certain independence of time, and it is possible that the thoughts of A some years ago can still be dealt with by the Producer and Stage Carpenter of B at the present day.

This would apply more particularly to persistent hauntings, which Tyrrell ascribes to the mind of the surviving deceased person, as he, or she, ruminates on some incident of the past. In neither case, of course, need it be said that the personal spirit returns.

There is also a reasonable theory for some hauntings, that, in a moment of crisis, some emotionally charged thought is pro-jected with such violence that it actually persists in the locality, ready to be picked up and perceived again by certain subjects. Generally, hauntings are connected with some strongly emotional experience, a murder or an act of violence; or sometimes with a strongly emotional attachment to a place or a thing, as a miser to his money. The atmosphere becomes charged with a certain attitude. Many people can sense atmospheres of this kind without seeing ghosts, and one knows ordinary people, who, on going into a house, even an empty house, can sense whether it has been a happy or an unhappy house.

On p. 33 we noticed Whately Carington's view of telepathy. On his Association theory, hauntings are accounted for by supposing that the buildings act as the associating object, and, when they are presented to another perceiving mind, this mind tends to pick up the ideas that the original mind associated with the buildings (*Telepathy*, 75–77). Suppose, for example, an elderly lady lives in my house, and I am accustomed to seeing her going up and down stairs. In fifty years time someone else will be living here, and this person may have the capacity of Eidetic Imagery, which is the ability to see a mental image as though it was an objective reality. From time to time, this person, looking at the stairs, will catch my associated idea of "stairs—old lady," and instead of merely finding the idea "old lady" inexplicably coming into his mind, he will actually see the figure of the old lady on the stairs.

A weakness of Carington's view here is that if a ghost is seen by several people together, it means that all of them have this gift of eidetic imagery, which is not common. Although Carington decries the influence of emotion on telepathy (p. 78), many hauntings have some strong emotional attachment, and it is likely that emotional conflict, realized or unrealized, can give power to certain mental patterns. This is borne out by hauntings that are accompanied by physical manifestations. Tyrrell in *Apparitions* touches on these only incidentally, and refers them to the realm of poltergeists, with which he is not dealing, and to which neither his nor Carington's theories are intended to apply. Elsewhere, however, Tyrrell has discussed physical phenomena, *e.g. The Personality of Man*.

POLTERGEISTS

The word Poltergeist comes from the German, and means "Noisy spirit." It is applied to manifestations in which objects are moved or thrown, and the poltergeist may be associated either with a locality, or with a person, frequently, though not always, with a young unmarried person of the age of puberty. Several modern books on this subject have appeared, including *Poltergeists over England*, by Harry Price (*Country Life*, 1945); *Poltergeists*, by Sacheverell Sitwell (Faber, 1940), and *The Story of the Poltergeist down the Centuries*, by Hereward Carrington and Nandor Fodor (Rider, 1953).

It must be said that many poltergeist happenings have proved to be fraudulent. Many others, however, have no normal explanation, and there are basic similarities in records from different ages and from different countries that make it likely that we are dealing

with some consistent supernormal phenomena. Two frequent
happenings in such cases are stone throwing and outbreaks of fire.

It is strange that some of the cases have occurred in the houses
of ministers. Epworth parsonage had a poltergeist when John
and Charles Wesley were children, and John Wesley himself wrote
an account of it. The children named it "Old Jeffery," and it used
to knock on the wall, especially during prayers, open doors, draw
curtains, etc. Here it is probable that the girl, Hetty Wesley,
was the unwitting centre of the disturbances. The Curé d'Ars was
also a well-known victim of poltergeist manifestations.

Often objects have been thrown about, or stones have flown
through the air, when no one has been there to throw them. They
have on occasions passed through holes too small to admit them
normally. Furniture has been moved about and crockery smashed.
Where stones or other objects have been seen in motion, they have
often appeared to the observer to be moving comparatively slowly.
It is not usual for anyone to be injured by a flying object, though
there have been occasional exceptions, as at Borley Rectory.

There would appear to be two possible ways of accounting for
the phenomena. The first is adopted by Dr. Nandor Fodor, who
has had experience of treating psychologically several of the centres
of poltergeistic phenomena. In the book which he has written
in collaboration with Dr. Hereward Carrington, he reprints a paper
that he gave before the Association for the Advancement of Psycho-
therapy, in 1945, and describes his investigation of a certain poltergeist victim, a married woman who, in his opinion, was suffering
from a serious state of dissociation. Careful analysis revealed the
likelihood of a severe shock at an early age, which now had brought
about a maladjusted attitude to life in general and to her husband
in particular. Dr. Fodor's conclusion is that the poltergeist is
not a ghost, but a bundle of projected repressions. One assumes
from this that a cluster of ideas, or psychon system, in the unconscious has the power to break out into a storm violent enough to
affect material objects. It is apparently another extreme form of
Psycho-Kinesis. One is reminded also of the wooden bench that
split in two when a psychological conflict was being resolved
(p. 111). The other way of accounting for the phenomena is to
suppose that evil spirits are at work. In favour of this is the fact
that these activities are never for the good of anybody: they are
disruptive and destructive. Yet the two explanations are not
necessarily mutually exclusive. Since one person is commonly
the storm-centre, it is possible that the spirits make use of some
vital force, frequently connected with sex development, which
they can materialize sufficiently to move other material objects. It
would be a kind of physical sublimation of the sex instinct.

THEORIES OF HAUNTINGS

Physical hauntings of a locality are apparently different, since they do not depend upon one individual. They may persist over a long period of time, and do not manifest only when a certain individual is present or in the neighbourhood. The hauntings at Borley Rectory would be in this category, though many happenings there resembled poltergeistic activity. Here objects of all kinds were thrown about, writing appeared on the walls, and eventually the house was mysteriously burnt down in 1941. Evidence for the phenomema was alleged to come from 200 witnesses, as recorded by Harry Price in *The Most Haunted House in England* (Longmans Green) and *The End of Borley Rectory* (Harrap), but his reliability has been under a cloud since the publication in 1956 of *The Haunting of Borley Rectory* by Eric Dingwall, Kathleen Goldney, and Trevor Hall (Duckworth).

A *simple* theory to explain all the phenomena is impossible in the present stage of our knowledge. Any theory is bound to sound fantastic. The theory of a returned spirit, or spirits, of former occupants of the house is no simpler than the theory of malicious non-human spirits or demons. In either case one has to find a bridge between spirit and matter to enable them to function. This bridge might be "mind-force" similar to that which operates in P.K. But is it the mind-force of the spirit itself, or the mind-force of former occupants, generated years ago, but transcending time and so still a force to be reckoned with today? Could this projection of mind operate in its own right, as it were? Since it appears to operate in relation to present-day observers, it seems more likely that it is being used by entities who are existing on the spot and are able to direct it. It is, however, just possible—however unlikely it appears—that by reason of its precognitive capacities, the mind of A, existing a century ago, has taken account of present-day investigators, and operates P.K. effects, not in relation to 100 years ago, but in relation to the present day. One assumes that the mind in question is likely to have been an evil one, and its effects have arisen from an evil cluster of ideas that had embedded itself in the unconscious. One remembers that experimental ESP and P.K. produce more significant results when the conscious mind is relaxed and not concentrating, *i.e.* the force flows from the unconscious rather than the conscious.

TRAVELLING CLAIRVOYANCE

When a ghost of a living person is seen, the original of the ghost is commonly unaware of the actions of the people to whom the ghost

appears. He is active in his own surroundings, and is not aware
of travelling in any astral body. But there are some cases in which
a subject, in light trance, or in sleep, has travelled to a distant
place, seen some person there, and has in turn been seen by him.

One of the most famous of such cases is recorded originally in
Proceedings of the S.P.R., Vol. VII, No. 41, but has often been
quoted (*e.g.* Tyrrell, *Apparitions*, 116 f.). A Mr. Wilmot, crossing
the Atlantic, shared a cabin with a friend. One night he dreamed
that his wife came into the cabin in her nightdress, hesitated on
seeing that he was not alone, but then moved in and kissed him.
On waking he was rebuked by his friend, who told him that, while
lying awake, he had seen a lady come in and kiss him. In due
course Mr. Wilmot arrived home, only to be asked by his wife
whether he had seen her "a week ago Tuesday." She then said
that she had been anxious about him, and during the night she
thought that she travelled out across the sea, came to a ship, and
went into a cabin. There she saw a man staring at her; but her
husband was also there asleep, and she went over and kissed him.
She accurately described the cabin, which was of an unusual
design.

This is certainly an extraordinary case, and it is tempting to
account for it by the theory of astral projection (pp. 78 ff.). Certainly
Tyrrell's "Producer" and "Stage Carpenter" have to work over-
time to account for it! Perhaps we can leave them to arrange
the appearance of the "ghost" in this case, but not eliminate here
the exercise of clairvoyance which transcends space and, if necessary,
time. Clairvoyance takes various forms: sometimes it sees things
as they are, sometimes it sees symbols: sometimes it sees things
that are virtually 100 per cent accurate, sometimes there is a large
or small amount of error mixed with truth. Mrs. Wilmot's mind
on this occasion perceived distant conditions with 100 per cent
accuracy, and clairvoyance on her part was combined with the
psychic paraphernalia that usually goes to make up the drama of
a ghost, if Tyrrell is correct.

What then is a ghost? Probably in most cases it is a harmless
thought-form. It may appear when its subject is passing through
a crisis, or about the time of death. We can regard it as genuine,
even though in a sense it is "not really there." Our conscious
mind becomes aware of it through responses that we normally
associate with the senses of seeing, hearing, or touch. This type
of ghost leaves no trace of its presence when it disappears.

Where physical effects are left, the ghost is of a more dangerous
kind, since these effects are rarely beneficial. We are face to face
either with a semi-materialized mind-force, that arises from a disorganized personality, living or dead, or with the activities of an
evil spirit entity. As a Christian one must stand in the Name of

Jesus Christ, and, where one person seems to be the storm centre, try to release the conflict that is probably there; though this will normally be the task of the psychiatrist.

CHAPTER XI

MAN AND HIS UNSEEN NEIGHBOURS

ONE of the marks of man's pride is the belief that he is the highest of all created beings. So far as the visible world is concerned, the Bible would agree with him. But there is no reason at all to suppose that there are no unseen beings between him and God. Indeed the Bible, from its earliest records to its latest, assures us of the existence of angels. Those who accept the documents of the Pentateuch according to the Wellhausen divisions, recognize that in Jacob's dream at Bethel, belonging to the alleged J & E strata, the angels of God ascend and descend on the ladder set up from earth to heaven (Gen. 28: 12). From time to time in the Old Testament some man of God is given a message by an angel, or sees a vision of God attended by a court of heavenly beings (e.g. Isa. 6). An angel announced to the Virgin Mary that she should be the mother of the Messiah (Luke 1: 26 f.). Jesus Himself spoke several times of the angels in heaven. Peter in Acts 12: 7 was released from prison by an angel. And the Book of the Revelation continually pictures the worship and work of the angels.

Yet angels have fared badly at the hands of men. Sometimes they have been regarded as semi-mediators between God and man, and as eligible to receive worship and prayer. Scripture is emphatic against such a practice (Col. 2: 18; Rev. 22: 8, 9), though it is one of the customs of Roman Catholicism.

For Evangelicals there has been the opposite error of ignoring the ministry of angels. The Evangelical centres his thoughts upon immediate contact with God, in and through Christ, and he is aware of the indwelling of the Holy Spirit. Angels therefore are difficult to fit into his theological scheme, though he accepts the fact of their existence.

The "modern" mind, both Christian and non-Christian, on the other hand, frequently disposes of angels altogether. It attributes many of the ideas in the Old Testament to pagan sources, and then falls into the well-known error of concluding that, by accounting for the origins of a thing, one has disproved its real existence.

The belief in demons has had a somewhat similar fate. The first definite statement about a fall of angels in Scripture comes in Gen. 6: 2, where "the sons of God" intermarried with the "daughters of men." We shall return to the interpretation of this later. From time to time we read of evil spirits, like the one that afflicted Saul in I Sam. 16: 14. The figure of a supreme Satan, or adversary, emerges in I Chron. 21: 1; Job 1: 2; and Zech. 3: 1, 2, and he and many demons contest the coming of the Kingdom through Christ, and carry on the warfare in the early Church. Paul regards them as our enemies in the Christian warfare. They are "the principalities, the powers, the world-rulers of this darkness, the spiritual hosts of wickedness in the heavenly places" (Eph. 6: 12). Their aim is to deceive, and there are several warnings to Christians to be on their guard against their cleverness (e.g. I Tim. 6: 1–3).

On the whole, in post-Biblical times demons have met with more respect than have the angels. Man is really very much afraid of the unseen world, and a demon can objectify that fear. Roman Catholics and Evangelicals both recognize the existence and the power of demons, but normally the former will use such instruments as holy water and the sign of the Cross as protection, while the Evangelical will claim the power of the precious Blood of Christ, and the authority of His Name as the Risen and Ascended Lord. There have indeed been devout Christians who appear to have been over-obsessed by the idea of demons and have gone beyond the New Testament balance. But the "modern mind" again has frequently abandoned Satan and demons, and supposes that modern psychology has accounted for everything that the Bible and orthodox Christians have ascribed to them.

There is, unfortunately, insufficient space to review in detail the Biblical references to angels and demons. There is little doubt that Jesus Christ treated them as personal entities, and we have no right to maintain that on this point He used the language of accommodation, fitting His words and actions to the beliefs of the people of His day. Most of us would agree that such a belief is of great spiritual importance, and ought to have been corrected if it was false, just as Christ corrected the false beliefs of the disciples that a man born blind was so born because of his parents' sin or because of his own in a previous life (John 9: 1–3). Nor can we seriously believe that on such a point as this our Lord was Himself ignorant. Even if there were any truth in the so-called Kenosis (self-emptying) theory, it could not be extended to cover Christ's knowledge of the heavenly world without jeopardising the whole of the revelation of God which He came to give.

ANGELS

In this chapter it must be sufficient to consider the relevance for mankind of the belief in angels and demons. The word translated "angel," both in Hebrew and in Greek, can be, and often is, translated "Messenger." The name thus indicates the chief function of the angels in relation to this world. They are messengers of God; and the Epistle to the Hebrews sums up their character in 1: 14: "Are they not all ministering spirits, sent forth to do service for the sake of them who shall inherit salvation?" A review of their appearances in the Bible shows that they do not act on their own initiative, but as directly commissioned by God. What Gabriel says of himself in Luke 1: 19 would be typical of any angelic messenger, "I am Gabriel, who stand in the presence of God; and I was sent to speak unto thee." In their mission they are thus completely God-centred, as indeed they are in their worship, of which a picture is given in Rev. 4 and 5.

Many speculations have been made about their nature. In Job 1: 6; 2: 1; 28: 7, and probably Gen. 6: 2, they are called "sons of God" (*Bene Elohim*). According to Hebrew idiom this could mean "gods"; for "sons of" expresses participation in. Thus "sons of the prophets" means "members of the prophetic order," and "a son of Belial" means "a wicked man." Moreover there is the interesting verse in Psa. 8: 5, which says that man has been made "a little lower than *Elohim*." The R.V. translates this last word in the normal way as "God," but the Greek Septuagint, followed by Heb. 2: 7, translates it as "angels." Of course either translation expresses what is true in fact. Man is made in the likeness of God, but in the gradation of spiritual and material beings he also comes a little lower than the angels. The word *Elohim* is a non-exclusive term for God. While it is frequently used of the true God, Jehovah, it is also used of the gods of the heathen, as in fact I have used the English word "god" in this very sentence. If it conveyed primarily the idea of "Supernatural Being" one can see how it would be used both of the Supreme Deity, and also of lesser supernatural beings, even of a spirit at a séance, as in I Sam. 28: 13, where the medium says "I see *Elohim* coming up out of the earth."

At the same time one cannot exclude the possibility that the title "Sons of God" is used of the angels to indicate that each is an independent creation of God: they do not give birth to one another by marriage (Matt. 22: 30). There is a basic connexion between the uses of "Son of God" in Scripture, which indicates what we may term an immediate experience of a "begetting" act of God. Thus it is used supremely of Jesus Christ, the eternally begotten Son of the Father. It is used of Adam in Luke 3: 38, inasmuch as he was a direct creation of God. It is used, not of all mankind, but of those who have been born again by the direct action of the Holy Spirit, as, for example, in John 1: 12, 13; Rom. 8: 15–17. And it is used of the angels, as we have seen.

Whichever interpretation is given to the angelic title, we know that angels are created beings, like ourselves, and we are told that they were already in existence before this world was formed, since God tells Job that, when He laid the foundations of the earth, the morning stars sang together, and all the sons of God shouted for joy (Job 38: 6, 7). Most people would agree, whether or not they believe these words in Job, that, if there are angels at all, they were probably in existence before man. As to their nature, it is called "spirit" in Heb. 1: 14. When we say "spirit" we commonly mean that which has its existence on a non-material plane. In man spirit manifests in a material body-mind relationship, but we can have a conception of spirit that manifests in a mind-relationship without the necessity of incarnation. What the capacities of such a spirit-mind would be, we cannot tell, since it is an order of being that we have not yet experienced. But it would be fair to regard angels as spirit-intelligences of that order. Man, bounded by that which links him to the material order, is more limited, and so "a little lower than the angels," but he is less limited, and so higher, than the rest of the animal world.

It is not easy to find authenticated evidence for the appearance of angels today, but after all, even in the Bible they appear only at rare intervals. From time to time there are stories from the mission field of protection by angels, but usually such stories are second or third hand by the time they are reported. But I know a small girl who in one of the London Blitzes told her mother that she had been very frightened until an angel came and sat at the foot of her bed. She is absolutely convinced that she did see an angel.

The most famous controversy of modern times has centred in the angels of Mons, who are supposed to have been seen by many soldiers in France during the early days of the 1914 War. Arthur Machen in his book *The Bowmen*, claimed that the legend arose from a fictitious story which he himself wrote in 1914. The idea came to him in church. He is answered by Harold Begbie in a book, *On the side of the Angels*, in which he produces witnesses who claim to have seen the angels. He suggests that Arthur Machen received the idea for the story by a telepathic awareness of the actual fact. My own inclination is to accept Begbie's evidence, but this may be wishful thinking. Both books are worth reading, but they are long since out of print, and are hard to come by. My copies are rare prizes from bookshop junk shelves at 6d. each.

DEMONS

From the good spirits we turn to the bad. The Christian Church follows its Master in accepting the existence of the Supreme Adversary, Satan. It is often asserted that the Jewish Satan arises from Zoroastrian dualism, where the supreme God of ultimate light and goodness, Mazda, is in conflict with the supreme God of darkness and sin, Ahriman. The original beliefs of Zoroastrianism are far from clear, but if we grant that the Jews came in contact with these ideas during the exile, it is by no means certain that their belief in Satan was influenced by them. Satan in the pages of Scripture is such an unusual figure that he is most unlikely to have been the product of invention, imagination, or absorption from others. In fact it is probably true that even the average Christian has a picture of Satan which is different from that of the Bible.

The existence and character of Satan may well be the subject of precise revelation. There is a remarkable consistency about him from the moment of his first appearance by name and up to the end of the Bible. Satan is first named in the prologue of the Book of Job, where he comes with the angels into the presence chamber of God, and, after making accusations about Job's genuineness of character, obtains permission to attack Job up to a certain point fixed by God. He does precisely the same, according to Jesus Christ, shortly before the crucifixion. If we follow the R.V. margin of Luke 22: 31, 32, our Lord says to Peter, "Simon, Simon, behold, Satan obtained you (plural) by asking that he might sift you as wheat: but I made supplication for thee (singular) that thy faith fail not." In the closing Book of the Bible (Rev. 12: 7–11) Satan is cast out of heaven, and is called "the accuser of our brethren, who accuses them before our God day and night."

Here is no picture of an absolute source of Evil, corresponding to an absolute Source of Good. The Bible, in disclosing the existence of Satan, is not dualistic. Who would have invented the idea of Satan having access to heaven? Yet this is part and parcel of the early Christian faith, as is seen in the extraordinary statement in Eph. 6: 12, that the Christian fights against evil powers "in the heavenly places." The phrase, "the heavenly places," is used earlier in the same Epistle for the sphere where the ascended Christ is enthroned in power (1: 20) and for the sphere of our blessing in Him (1: 3; 2: 6).

THE NATURE OF EVIL

But if Satan is not the absolute source of evil, what relationship does he bear to evil? To answer this we must try to visualize what is meant by evil and sin. Is it a positive thing, existing in its own right, or a negative thing, an absence of good? To say that it is a positive thing is to say, either that evil has an eternal existence, or that God created evil. If the former is true, we have the dualistic idea of an eternally good God, eternally confronted by an eternal opposite. The latter might seem to harmonize with Isa. 45: 7, where God says, "I make peace, and create evil," but the parallel of peace, shows that "evil" here is used in the sense of "disaster," as in Zeph. 1: 12 and Amos 3: 6. To say that God brought positive evil into existence would impugn His righteousness.

Yet evil appears to be positive in character, and more than negative. We must realize that there is a distinction between the essential act of sin, which is negative rebellion, and the evil consequences that follow, which certainly are positive. A creature who is given freedom of will must *ipso facto* have the capacity to say No to his Creator. So long as he says Yes, he functions as the creature that he was meant to be: he is positively good. But suppose that he exercises his freedom, and says No, the negative refusal does not end there. It sets up a chain of reactions that disorganize the nature, and this disorganization is positively bad. The Garden of Eden story illustrates this perfectly. The initial sin of disobedience set in motion a chain of factors that now made for death instead of life. Or one may take the analogy of a machine that is running perfectly as the maker planned, because all the parts are in perfect alignment. If one small part slips out of alignment, and the power continues to drive the machine, the negative slip will become positive destruction, as other parts readjust themselves in view of the initial wrong alignment.

Fallen Angels

Since we cannot suppose that Satan has an eternal existence, nor that he was created evil, we presume that he was created free, as man was, and that he fell through disobedience as man did. To ask why God created Satan and man if He knew that they would sin, is to ask an unanswerable question. If a free being is a better companion than a machine, and God, in deliberately choosing to create, wished to create beings who could have fellowship with Himself, we presume that He would create free beings. If you are a parent, would you choose to have a ventriloquist's doll, or a child who may break your heart? The question why God created beings who would ultimately fall may well be a foolish question, if it means that we are demanding that God should do two contradictory things at the same time; namely, create free beings who are not free.

The Bible indicates that Satan and other spirits have fallen, just as man has fallen. Yet there are two groups of fallen spirits. One group, as we have seen, have a certain freedom, and are in active rebellion against God and His people. Yet others are spoken of as in prison (II Pet. 2: 4; Jude 6).

We have not so far attempted to distinguish between one type of evil spirit and another. The Bible indicates that there are grades, and speaks of principalities and powers, and spiritual hosts of wickedness (Eph. 6: 12). In particular there are those who are called demons (Gk. *Daimonion*). The A.V. mistranslates this as "devil," but the Greek of the New Testament reserves the term Devil (*Diabolos*) for Satan: it is always in the singular. Nothing is said as to the origin of these demons. As to their nature, Christ refers to them as "spirits"; when the disciples rejoice that "even the demons are subject to us in Thy name," He tells them not to rejoice primarily in this, "that the spirits are subject unto you" (Matt. 10: 17, 20). It is perhaps simplest to regard them as those who fell at first with Satan.

DEMON POSSESSION

Demon possession demands serious consideration. It has been accepted as a fact by most nations from early times, and is still recognized today. It was apparently accepted by Jesus Christ, and many of the cures that He and His disciples practised were based on the real existence of demons which had to be cast out. Jesus and His disciples distinguished clearly between normal physical illnesses, that were cured generally by the laying on of hands or anointing with oil, and those cases of possession which were cured by the word of command (*e.g.* Matt. 10: 8; Mark 6: 13; Luke 13: 32), even though these latter cases often showed the symptoms of ordinary diseases such as dumbness and blindness (Matt. 9: 32, 33; 12: 22).

The chief characteristic of demon possession appears to have been the control of the body of the possessed in an abnormal way, against what was believed to be the will of the person. Where the possessing spirit was prepared to speak, it spoke of itself as an entity different from the man it was possessing. Thus the spirits in Mark 5 recognized Jesus for what He was, and gave their name as Legion.

Similar characteristics have been noted in recent times from various parts of the world, and they have attracted particular notice in China. The stories may lack the amount of corroboration in detail that we should desire, but their similarity in general outline, as they come from different parts, makes them inherently likely. A person suddenly exhibits another personality, and speaks in a different voice, which Miss Mildred Cable describes as "the weird minor chant of the possessed, the voice, as in every case I have seen, clearly distinguishing it from insanity" (*The Fulfilment of a Dream*, p. 118). The person often becomes violent, and may exhibit supernatural knowledge. Usually his words are evil, and often blasphemous.

A very full study of cases in China was made by a missionary, Dr. J. L. Nevius, in 1892, in *Demon Possession and Allied Themes* (Fleming H. Revell). Although this book is often quoted, it is not easy to find a copy today; but those who can discover one should certainly read it. Dr. Nevius began his studies with a detailed questionnaire, which he sent to many missionaries and Chinese Christians, so as to discover as much first-hand information as possible. His conclusion in the light of all the evidence is that demon possession is what the name suggests, and it cannot be equated with any ordinary physical or psychological derangement.

There is, however, the alternative view that all alleged cases of demon possession can be removed from the sphere of the supernatural, and regarded as examples of dissociation of a human personality. A full book on these lines is by T. K. Oesterreich, whose German work is published in English under the title of *Possession, Demoniacal and Other, among Primitive Races, in Antiquity, the Middle Ages, and Modern Times* (Kegan Paul, 1930). This is a book of nearly 400 pages, and is a well-documented work with examples drawn from all ages and countries. Oesterreich maintains that the equivalents of possession today among civilized peoples are "a particularly extensive complex of compulsive phenomena, which naturally exist in great numbers today, every marked nervous state habitually bringing them in its train. But these processes do not now develop with the same ease as formerly when the auto-suggestion of possession supervened" (p. 124).

This means that, if a person believes in possession by demons, he will tend to ascribe certain unpleasant mental states to possession, instead of realizing that they are the products of his own mind which should be treated as such. He will thus externalize the conflict, and suffer a more definite splitting of his personality. There is also a voluntary form of possession, in which a person deliberately seeks to be controlled by a spirit. But Oesterreich is emphatic that in all forms of possession there is only one Ego, "one single and identical subject which finds itself now in the normal, now in the abnormal state" (p. 38). The Ego in the abnormal state often possesses powers of telepathy and prediction, which are ascribed to the demon. But Oesterreich knows enough about parapsychology to see that this could be accounted for by the latent powers that are in the mind of man, quite apart from postulating demonic influence.

It is a pity that Oesterreich never read Dr. Nevius's book. He refers to it, but admits that he had never seen it. Some of the evidence that Nevius produces might well have modified his conclusions. It is curious also that Oesterreich has little to say about the extreme cases of dissociated personality. There have been certain famous cases in which a person has suddenly switched completely to an entirely different personality. The most fascinating treatment of such a case is without doubt Dr. Morton Prince's *The Dissociation of a Personality*. Here a somewhat gloomy and prim Miss Beauchamp was switched from time to time to a bright and lively second personality, who called herself Sally. Miss Beauchamp was wholly unaware of anything that Sally did while in occupation of the body, whereas Sally was aware of her predecessor's doings, so much so that she used to play tricks on her, and, while in temporary possession, she would smoke cigarettes (which Miss Beauchamp loathed) and hide her papers. Other secondary personalities emerged also. The fascination of the story lies in the decision which the psychiatrist had to make, as to which of the personalities he should try to fix. In spite of her "wickedness" Sally was so much more human than the other personalities. But I will not spoil the story for those who have not read it. There are other very similar cases, factual parallels to the Jekyll and Hyde of fiction.

The importance of these cases is the evidence that they supply for whole complexes of personality, which can be built up below the surface, ready to take over at a moment's notice. We are aware of normal manifestations of this: in the business world a man may be one personality; in his family life a different man altogether. Sometimes this leads to a most unsatisfactory state of affairs, where a man is a devout Christian in his Church life, but is merciless in his weekday life. Two unreconciled personalities in one may make him a hypocrite.

What one must decide is whether the modern psychological knowledge of complexes and split personalities has accounted for what was formerly believed to be demon possession. We may admit some cases, but need not admit all.

Perhaps the only proof would be the practical one. Christians, confronted with cases of demon possession, have, after fervent prayer, been able to command the demon to depart in the Name of Jesus Christ. The cure has generally been permanent, unless, as has sometimes happened in missionary lands, the person has gone back to idolatry. Can a case that involves an "extensive complex of compulsive phenomena" (to quote Oesterreich) be cured in this way? This is for a psychiatrist to say, but I think the answer would be No; otherwise more psychiatrists would be obtaining sudden cures: though, if they were not themselves Christians, they might be in the same danger as the sons of Sceva (Acts 19: 13–16)!

Certainly the casting out of demons is no light thing. We must be warned by the example of Christ. He was aware of the unseen world in a way that we are not. He spoke of the danger of the spirit returning to his former victim accompanied by other spirits also, unless the victim has in the meantime filled the house of his life with another Owner (Luke 11: 24–26). On the occasion when He cast out the legion of demons from the man by the sea, He let them go into the herd of swine, which thereupon rushed down into the sea. The moral difficulty is removed by realizing that Christ was well aware of the danger of releasing a mass of demons in the crowd. It may be relevant to refer to a case reported by John Layard in the *Proceedings of the S.P.R.*, Vol. XLVII, p. 237 (1944). When a patient under analytical treatment apparently reached the point of resolution of her conflict, a heavy wooden bench split down its entire length with a sudden loud report. Maybe it was coincidence: maybe it was something more, the exit of a demon.

THE METHOD AND MANNER OF POSSESSION

One would surmise that the place of possession by an evil spirit (to use inadequate spatial terms) would be the spirit of man, which is the gateway to the spiritual world. This should be under the control of the Holy Spirit when it has been made alive with the new life of God. But if it is not used by its rightful Occupier, it may be used by another. It is also a control-centre for the whole of man's being. If it is merely empty, the being of man will either be unorganized, or organized round some inadequate centre. Unpleasant complexes may develop as a natural consequence, producing mental and physical symptoms. Possession by a demon may intensify these symptoms, and may also produce a flood of supernormal effects. The demon may seize on unpleasant personality groupings that are already forming, and emerge as a new personality in the person. If the case is genuine demon possession, the casting out of the demon in the Name of Jesus Christ will enable the normal personality to function again and the physical symptoms to disappear. Relief may also come through slow psychological treatment. If the patient can be brought to face up to the symptoms and to understand them to some extent, the hold of the demon will be lessened, and he may go. Even Christ recognized that demons could be cast out by others than Christians, when he asked the Jews, "If I by Beelzebub cast out demons, by whom do your sons cast them out?" (Luke 11: 19): and pagan religions agree that exorcism is possible.

Why should a demon wish to possess a person? There may be two reasons. Possession is part of the war against God and His people. It is significant that there were so many cases of possession in Palestine during the earthly ministry of Christ. Naturally Satan mobilized his forces there. But Jesus Christ continually defeated this opposition, and He has passed on the possibility of

victory to His Church.   Even a Christian atmosphere in a country
will lead to a lessening of the number of cases of possession, as it
has done in our own.

But it may also be that the demon himself gains something
from possession.   It gives him a body in which he can express
himself.   One recalls Gen. 6: 2.

It is not entirely fanciful to raise the question of national, as
well as personal, control.   A remarkable verse in Dan. 10: 13
speaks of "the prince of the kingdom of Persia," a spiritual being
who resisted the coming of an angel to bring a message to Daniel.
He is himself resisted by Michael, whom we hear later is one who
stands up for the Jews (Dan. 12: 1).

A similar idea is suggested in Psa. 82 which begins with the remarkable verse, "Elohim standeth in the congregation of El; He
judgeth among the Elohim."   Traditionally this Psalm has been
interpreted of God's calling of earthly rulers to account, but it is
more likely to be the judgment of angelic rulers, who are said to
have misruled the people over whom they had influence.   So
vers. 6, 7 declare "I said, ye are Elohim, and all of you sons of the
Most High.   Nevertheless ye shall die like men, and fall like one
of the princes."   This latter statement would be meaningless if
they were already men and princes.   This interpretation is not
negatived by Christ's quotation of ver. 6 in John 10: 34–36, since
He interprets the verse as applying to those "unto whom the word
of God came," *i.e.* those who are called to account by God in this
Psalm; leaving the question open as to whether they are men or
angels.   Christ's argument of course is that if the title "Elohim"
is applied in Scripture even to evil beings who exercise authority
under God, the title "Son of God" in its fullest sense can be assumed
by Him without blasphemy when His Divine mission is unique, and
His works declare that He is what He claims to be.

Further passages which suggest the national influence of evil
powers are found in both the Old and New Testaments.   We
have already noticed the power behind Babylon and Tyre.   In
Isaiah 24: 21, God finally punishes the "host of the high ones on
high, and the kings of the earth upon the earth."   And the Book
of the Revelation is shot through with the idea of evil spiritual
beings deceiving the nations *e.g.* 16: 13, 14.

There is no adequate reason for challenging these apocalyptic
ideas.   Even if one can see resemblances to pagan mythology,
particularly when Satan is referred to as Leviathan, the serpent and
the dragon (Isa. 27: 1; Rev. 12: 9), it is more than likely that the
pagan myth of primeval conflict between the Creator and Chaos
(in various forms) is simply a perversion of the actual fact of the
fall of Satan.

A fair deduction from all these passages is that our warfare on earth is part of a cosmic warfare. The rebellion of the angels was followed by the rebellion of the human race. Since the human race is the focal point of Christ's redemption, it is also the centre of the Satanic warfare directed against the kingdom of God. Michael and his angels are also engaged in the warfare, and there are grades of good and evil beings. Certainly there are good guardian angels for children (Matt. 18: 10), and there are good angels who stand by the churches (Rev. 1: 20). Evil spirits probably have a more roving commission, but there are some who are sufficiently powerful to sway the counsels of nations (Dan. 10: 13; Psa. 82). Here admittedly we face a great mystery, but one of the more puzzling features of international life is the way in which a country is somehow led into decisions that the vast majority of its members do not wish. There are, moreover, certain traits of national character that come out from generation to generation. One cannot attribute these things solely to the control of an evil national angel, but an acceptance of the Biblical view is at least suggestive.

One may take the further step and say that there is a reality behind the gods of the heathen. One can be a monotheist, and still believe this. This is not always realized by the theologians who trace the development of monotheism in the Old Testament. Moses could be as staunch a monotheist as Isaiah, even though the Decalogue says "Thou shalt have none other gods before me" (Ex. 20: 3). Canaanite gods and goddesses were not pure figments of the imagination, however fictitious the legends about them may be; but in them spirit entities were receiving the worship which belongs to the One God alone. Paul's words in 1 Cor. 8: 4–6 are to the same effect.

May it be that a Christian country is one in which the evil controlling angel has been supplanted by a good one? This comes about through the advance of the Christian Church in its warfare of prayer, evangelization, and instruction. The pattern of this warfare is that of Israel's invasion of Canaan, where the treatment of the enemy was ruthless. Our warfare on the hosts of darkness must be equally ruthless, though now the Bible has revealed to us the existence of the ultimate enemies, who use nations and individuals as their tools. That is why wars and conferences accomplish very little by themselves; they only patch up troubles. The one effective attack is prayer, the preaching of the Word of God, and putting on the whole armour of God, such as is set out in Eph. 6: 10–18. Unfortunately we are too ready to spare Satan, and even when we smite him with the Sword of the Spirit, we find him wounding us in return where we have forgotten to put on the whole armour of God.

CHAPTER XII

THE EVIDENCE FOR REINCARNATION

Most of the books and articles that have been written on reincarnation have faced the question from a philosophical, or semi-philosophical, point of view. From this standpoint the book by Canon Marcus Knight, *Spiritualism, Reincarnation, and Immortality* (Duckworth, 1950), has dealt very well with the subject. But apparently no Christian writer has attempted to examine the alleged evidence for reincarnation, and to offer some alternative explanation of the facts. Yet, after all our arguments we may be confronted with people who say that they can remember and can give proof of their memory of previous lives. This is what we must consider in this chapter.

A belief in reincarnation is part of the faith of some 230 million Hindus and 150 million Buddhists. It is held in a simpler form by many animistic peoples. In this country it is held by Theosophists, Anthroposophists, many Spiritualists, and others who are interested in the occult. Rudolf Steiner may be regarded as one of the most notable apostles of the belief in modern times. The survey, *Puzzled People*, a few years ago said that 10 per cent of believers in life after death held some theory of reincarnation. Pythagoras, Schopenhauer, Hegel, and Goethe, are amongst those who have held this belief, while amongst modern philosophers McTaggart and Macneile Dixon have been attracted to it. It is not therefore a childish belief that can lightly be set aside. There is much about it that is noble and extremely attractive to those who look for justice and order in the universe.

Let us see first of all what believers in reincarnation hold. Here one finds certain differences between them. Hinduism believes in the rebirth of individual souls. Hinayana Buddhism, and perhaps Gautama Buddha himself, denies the separate existence of the soul or self, but holds that a new bundle of qualities is created by the sum of the actions of the previous life. Both Hinduism and Buddhism accept the doctrine of Karma, which means *Deed*, *Act*, or *Work*. Karma is regarded as the underlying law of the universe, which no god or man can set aside. It is the law that whatever a man sows he must reap exactly. Thus our allotment of good or evil in this present life is precisely what we have merited in previous lives, no more and no less. Most of those in this country who accept reincarnation, accept the doctrine of Karma also.

A constructive presentation of the doctrine is to be found in Robert N. Kotzé's book, *The Scheme of Things* (Dakers, 1949), which combines the belief with a theory of evolution. He postulates the existence of a group-soul, "a psychic entity which ensouls a whole group of animals" (p. 42). In the earliest forms of life there would be one common psychic entity, but gradually different groups of creatures, partaking of this one group-soul, had different experiences, with the result that portions of their psychic existence could not merge into the main group-soul at death, but came together to form a new group-soul. The process continued, till one day "the portion of the group-soul incarnated in a single individual has experiences of such a nature that its temporary and incomplete division from the main body becomes permanent, and it can never again automatically reunite with it" (p. 45). This individual has now reached the Egoic stage, and has become a human being; henceforward it incarnates in one human body at a time. At first it develops by reincarnating quickly, but it comes to spend longer and longer in the psychic world. "Finally we reach the situation as we have it today, where it seems that the period of discarnate existence may stretch over hundreds of years" (p. 45). The ultimate end is "the merging of all perfected mankind into a single Divine Being" (p. 187). "The souls of all mankind, when perfected, instead of being reabsorbed into the bosom of Nirvana, may be fused together and merged into the transcendent consciousness of a new God. The consciousness of all of us might be used as the cells, so to say, for the body of a great new Divinity, who would be the final product of our evolution" (p. 159).

This is a magnificent theory, and the idea of group-souls may well be needed to account for such things as the guiding life-principle in colonies of bees, ants, and termites, as Eugene Marais has argued in *The Soul of the White Ant* (Methuen, 1937). But the evolution of this group-soul from animal to God is no more than pure speculation unless some tangible evidence can be produced to support it.

We turn then to look for evidence. It would seem that if there is evidence, it will be found in one or more of the following places:

1. It may be revealed by God, or by some discarnate spirits, as a fact. The reliability of such evidence will depend upon how far we are convinced of the authenticity of the alleged revelation.

2. Certain individuals may remember previous existences, and be able to furnish satisfactory proofs of what they say that they remember. There would not appear to be any other source of evidence than these two.

REVELATION

It is doubtful whether Hindus and Buddhists would regard their belief in reincarnation as dependent upon divine revelation. Their belief is rather part of their whole philosophy, which, they claim, can be proved by those who by means of the discipline of yoga tune themselves to the inner reality of the universe.

Christians naturally turn to the Bible to see whether reincarnation forms part of the revelation there. In particular they turn to the teachings of Jesus Christ. If reincarnation is a fact, it is obviously a fact of the most tremendous importance; it concerns man's eternal destiny. We are not therefore demanding that Our Lord should make a pronouncement on some interesting trifle. But we are saying that if the doctrine is true, He could not have ignored it, but must have made it part of His whole teaching.

It is however commonly stated that on one occasion Christ did teach reincarnation, when He referred to John the Baptist as "Elijah which was to come." The relevant passages are Matt. 11: 14; 17: 10–12; Mark 9: 11–13. We may, however, interpret Christ's words perfectly naturally in the light of Luke 1: 17, where the angel said that John would serve God "in the spirit and power of Elijah," not that he was actually Elijah in person. It is, in fact, impossible to hold that Christ meant that John was Elijah reincarnated, when the context of Matt. 17 is borne in mind. On the Mount of Transfiguration the disciples had just seen and heard Moses and Elijah, not Moses and John the Baptist; that is, Elijah in the other world still existed as Elijah. But even if John the Baptist was actually Elijah in person, we are dealing with something abnormal, since Elijah did not die like ordinary men. We should thus have an argument against reincarnation rather than in its favour; for the only example of reincarnation in Scripture would be that of a man who did not pass through the ordinary channel of death.

Other arguments from the Scriptures are based on superficial understanding. Thus there is no reference to reincarnation when the records speak about the Incarnation of Jesus Christ. Shaw Desmond's statement that "this great Master of Life and Death, like all created things, had had to pass through reincarnation after reincarnation" (p. 58) has no warrant in the words of Jesus Himself or in the New Testament as a whole. The Incarnation of Jesus Christ is the Incarnation of the Second Person of the Trinity, who emptied Himself of the glory which He had before the world was (Phil. 2: 6–11; John 17: 5).

To sum up: Scripture lends no support to the doctrine of re-incarnation. It speaks of this life now as the time of decision.

It goes so far as to say that "it is appointed unto men once to die" (Heb. 9: 27). In view of this it is difficult to hold even that the doctrine was an esoteric belief in the early Church. To anyone who believes that Jesus Christ was the incarnate Son of God, it is a striking point that He was not sent into the world as a Buddhist or a Hindu, in the stream of reincarnationist teaching, but He was born as a Jew, as the climax of a non-reincarnationist religion.

A discussion of how far a belief in reincarnation existed amongst Jews in the time of Christ, and amongst Christian and semi-Christian sects later, would demand more space than can be spared here. In his article in the *Encyclopaedia of Religion and Ethics* Dr. Gaster does not think that there is sufficient evidence to decide when reincarnationist ideas came to be held by some of the Jews. Gnostic sects soon after the time of Christ certainly held them.

One must, of course, distinguish between belief in reincarnation and belief in the pre-existence of the soul. Even the remark of the disciples in John 9: 2 might express no more than the suggestion that the man born blind had sinned in a previous existence as a soul, before he had been born into the world at all. A number of early Christian Fathers accepted the pre-existence—though not the pre-incarnation—of the soul, and reincarnationists, who quote them, do not always observe this distinction. Origen was a notable exponent of this view, and in a somewhat similar form the view has been stated in recent times by such theologians as Dr. N. P. Williams in *Ideas of the Fall and of Original Sin* (Longmans) and Canon Peter Green in a booklet, *The Pre-Mundane Fall* (Mowbray). These writers held a doctrine of a fall of a world soul, of which our souls are incarnated fragments.

Spiritualism

We suggested, however, that, if there was no revelation from God, there might be some revelation from discarnate spirits. Some have claimed that this is so, and that mediums have been the recipients of messages asserting that reincarnation is a fact.

The testimony of these messages is, however, considerably weakened by similar messages which assert that reincarnation is not a fact. Until recently it was generally true to say that spirit messages on the Continent supported reincarnation, while messages in this country denied it. Those who are critical of the spirit messages suggest that the reason for this was the influence of the tradition of Allan Kardec, who was one of the leading French spiritualists in the last century. In his book, *Le Livre des Esprits*, he quotes messages which teach a doctrine of reincarnation not unlike that of Kotzé.

Spiritualists and reincarnationists have explained these differences by saying that those who have passed over tend to retain
their habits of thought and outlook.   Thus a reincarnationist in
this life would still hold reincarnationist views in the life to come.
The reverse would also be true.   Dr. Alexander Cannon, in *Powers
That Be* (Rider), pp. 186 f., is particularly concerned because someone had obtained information from a high spirit that "under no
circumstances whatever does the soul come again to earth."   Dr.
Cannon suggests that the sitter had been misled.   He holds that
some people "get into touch with entities that have nothing valid
to impart, or they find themselves catching their own reflected
thoughts."

Obviously this robs the testimony of these communicators of
all their value, since the opinion of the discarnate communicator
has precisely the same value as the opinion that he held while on
earth.   Why should not Dr. Cannon himself be the one who is in
touch with entities that have nothing valid to impart?   Or why
should not he be catching his own reflected thoughts?

Clearly the supposed evidence from the spirit world is worthless
for discovering the truth about reincarnation, and most Theosophists and Anthroposophists pay little attention to the communications of spiritualism.

THE MEMORY OF PREVIOUS LIVES

It is admitted by everyone that only the minutest percentage
of people even profess to have a memory of a previous existence.
This absence of memory is regarded as one of the strongest arguments against reincarnation.   But the argument can be turned in
two ways.   First, it can be urged that memory is almost entirely
a faculty of the physical brain, and is connected primarily with
bodily experiences.   Each body will then build up its own train
of memories, and will not inherit the memories that belonged to
the brains of former existences.   This is the line taken by Dr.
Kolisko, though he believes that under certain conditions memories
of past lives can be brought up from the subconscious.

The other way of turning the argument is to point out the
necessity of forgetfulness if the reincarnated soul is ever to develop
fresh experiences.   This is Kotzé's explanation, and it appears
reasonable.   Whatever new set of circumstances may fall to my
lot in this life, I can never face them with an entirely fresh sheet.
I must face them with the accumulated habits, outlook, and personality, that have become an inevitable part of myself during the
years.   Thus, if I were to be launched into a fresh incarnation with
all the memories of this life, my growth in experience would be
considerably hampered.

Yet it is claimed that by some freak of nature, or by deliberate training, some people have been able to remember incidents from their past lives. It is not easy, however, to find well-documented cases. Mostly writers refer to certain instances, often giving names, and perhaps assuring us that they have investigated them. But anyone who has followed cases of alleged apparitions' and communications in the records of the Society for Psychical Research, knows how easy it is to have a convincing hearsay story that dwindles to very small proportions once it is thoroughly investigated.

But a few cases have been given in greater detail. Ralph Shirley, in *The Problem of Rebirth*, quotes one that appears to be well authenticated. It is the case of Alexandrina Samona, and is vouched for by Alexandrina's father, who was a well-known doctor in Sicily, by Count Ferdinand Monroy de Ranchibile of Palermo, by a Protestant Pastor at Palermo, and by others whose names and titles are given.

The case is briefly as follows: On March 15, 1910, Dr. Samona lost his little daughter, Alexandrina, aged about five, through meningitis. Three days later the mother dreamed that Alexandrina appeared and said that she would come back "little." The dream was repeated, but the mother ignored it, since, owing to an operation, it seemed impossible that she could ever have another child. A little later the family, while discussing the dreams, heard three loud knocks on the door, though no one was there. They determined to hold a séance, in the course of which Alexandrina purported to communicate, and assured her parents that she would be born again before Christmas. At further séances the message came that a baby sister would be born at the same time. After about three months the communications ceased, since the alleged Alexandrina said that she would now have to pass into a state of sleep.

On November 22 twin daughters were born, and one of them, as she grew older, proved to be very like Alexandrina, both physically and mentally. Her twin, on the other hand, was completely different.

At eight years old Alexandrina II described a visit to a certain Church that she had never seen, whereas Alexandrina I had been there shortly before her death. Amongst other things she said, "We went there with a lady who had horns, and met with some little red priests in the town." In fact they had gone with a lady who had certain disfiguring excrescences on her forehead, and had met a group of young Greek priests with blue robes decorated with red ornamentation.

A comparison of the dates indicates either that the birth of Alexandrina II was premature, or that the "soul" of Alexandrina I did not enter the body for some time after its conception.

There are several similar stories in this chapter. Shaw Desmond in Chapter XI has a case of a different nature from India, for which he says that he has some corroborative details from the head-master and two other masters of the Government school. In this instance Vishwa Nath, born on February 7, 1921, in Bareilly, began at the age of one-and-a-half to give minute details of his previous life in Pilibhit. On being taken a little later to Pilibhit, he pointed out "himself" in a group photo, and thus established his identity as Laxmi Narain, who had died on December 15, 1918.

Where the alleged memory is fairly general, one may safely ascribe it to suggestion. Eric Cuddon, in *Hypnosis, its meaning and practice* (G. Bell), gives an experiment in which he suggested to a subject under hypnosis that she had been the favourite slave of the Emperor Nero, and had been taken by him on a trip to Egypt. Although she had no conscious recollection of the suggestion, on being asked a week later whether she had lived before, she replied that she was quite certain that she had been the favourite slave of the *Egyptian* Emperor Nero. Several people have called attention to the fact that quite a number of women "remember" having been Marie Antoinette. I myself can "remember" the sensation of taking off in an aeroplane, though I have never tra-velled by plane in my life, and certainly did not do so in a previous incarnation.

When we come to more definite and provable memories, there are one or two points to be taken into consideration. There is, for example, the faculty of psychometry, whereby a person who has certain gifts can take an object, and by contact with it can tell facts about the past and future of its owner, or others who have handled it. It is *as though* experiences have an objective existence, and continue in some form in which they can be picked up, and partially relived, by those who are tuned in to them (p. 47). Many people, who have no such gift, are familiar with the experience of sensing the atmosphere of even an empty house, and are able to say that the house has had a happy or a gloomy history.

One might also raise the evidence of certain dreams. Ralph Shirley in Chapter VI gives some examples of dreams in which the dreamer seemed to be transported back into a previous exist-ence. His next chapter concerns dream travelling in the present and future, when the dreamer dreams repeatedly of some unknown house to which he or she later goes to live. In one or two cases the dreamer is seen as a ghost by the people living in the house at the time of the dream. I have referred to this sort of dream on p. 44.

We thus have to face the whole question of the relation of the unconscious to time and space. If the dreamer can on occasions transcend the normal conditions of space, it is equally possible that he can on occasions transcend the normal conditions of time also. The quiet of sleep might release on these occasions something like psychometric powers, so that the dreamer becomes tuned in to some occasion of the past. But if this can happen in sleep, it might also happen to people of a particular type even when they were awake, giving them the conviction that they had actually lived in the past themselves.

This would be somewhat similar to the experience of Miss Moberly and Miss Jourdain, who went back into the past at Versailles, and who met people of 1789, including one who appeared to be Marie Antoinette. (See p. 58 f.).

I have already mentioned the part that Marie Antoinette plays in "memories" of previous incarnations, and there may be a clue here to the explanation of these memories of the past. Many of them concern some strongly emotional situation. The same is true of hauntings of places. May it not be that a powerful emotional disturbance throws off some element which lingers in space and time, and which can be sensed by certain people under certain conditions? The tragic situation of Marie Antoinette is one such emotional condition. A battle for life and death in the Roman arena, such as Shaw Desmond remembers, is another.

On p. 33 we mentioned Mr. Whately Carington's arguments for the existence of what he calls *Psychon Systems*. He maintains that a thought-system, which is the product of someone's thinking, may exist in its own right; and, in the presence of some link that is common to the original thinker and the new percipient, it may pass into the consciousness of the new percipient. Whately Carington incidentally connects his theory with the theory of reincarnation, and in particular with the fact of sudden genius, which is often urged as a strong argument for reincarnation. Briefly, he holds that the mental work done by previous researchers may often be the source of those sudden ideas that flash into the minds of people doing similar work today (*Telepathy*, pp. 141, 42). If this is true, it would account for such a fact as the Glastonbury scripts.

One cannot therefore rule out the possibility of unconscious telepathy in the case of Alexandrina Samona. The resemblance of the two Alexandrinas is no more than occurs in a fair proportion of families when the children are under the age of five. In this case the problem might appear to be increased by the fact that the coming of Alexandrina II was announced beforehand. But since it is almost impossible to deny that certain people, including mediums, have a genuine gift of seeing into the future (whatever the explanation may be), the preliminary announcement of Alexandrina's return does not in itself throw any light on whether the child who was born was in fact Alexandrina.

Other experiences, such as that of the Indian boy, are, even according to the reincarnationist hypothesis, so rare that they must be due to something abnormal in the make-up of the child. The abnormality might consist in an unconscious linking-up with another mind, in this special case with someone living at Pilibhit. The thoughts that this person had of the deceased Laxmi Narain then became a part of the thoughts of the child Vishwa Nath. This would not be anything essentially different from the employment of clairvoyant powers, though where an adult clairvoyant could distinguish between his actual life and the thoughts and experiences of others received clairvoyantly or telepathically, a child might not so distinguish.

Conclusion

To the ordinary man in the street these explanations may appear so strange that it would seem far simpler to accept reincarnation as a fact. As a Christian I feel bound to look for some other explanation than the superficial one. This explanation is not so strange in the light of the facts of telepathy and clairvoyance, and of the workings of the human mind at its deep levels. The explanation ought not to seem strange to believers in reincarnation also, since the majority of them speak of what they call the *Akashic World Record*. This term expresses the belief that all the events of the world are somehow impressed upon material objects or, alternatively, exist in a world of time which is not successive but contemporaneous. A person with the special sense developed can perceive these events. I quote this belief, not as accepting it myself, but as an *argumentum ad hominem*. On the reincarnationist's own hypothesis, it seems to me to offer an alternative explanation for the apparent memory of previous lives; these memories need be no more than the picking up of fragments of the world memory.

CHAPTER XIII

THE BIBLICAL VIEW OF MAN

THE time has come to try to build up a constructive picture of man's being. As we have followed through facts and theories in the previous chapters, we have occasionally noticed how they may be related to, or come into conflict with, the Biblical teaching. In this chapter we must consider the Biblical view itself, as constituting a positive basis for a proper understanding of man.

The Books of the Bible cover many centuries of time. Revelation in these books is progressive, in the sense that every aspect of truth was not revealed at once, but that fresh truths were unfolded from age to age and from writer to writer. One might compare progressive revelation to the classification of some object as one approaches it through mist and swirling cloud. It may be a pony that is standing on a patch of grass on a mountain. At first we see a mass that we declare to be an animal's body. After a few steps we see a head and legs. If the pony stays still long enough, we soon distinguish its shade of colour; and finally we can see every mark on it.

Progressive revelation is sometimes used in a different sense, as though we first declare that we see a pile of stones, then, on coming nearer, we wonder whether it is a bush. Then the object takes shape as an animal, which we suspect to be a cow; and only at the end we find to our surprise that it is a pony. According to the first view, the Bible goes steadily forward in truth; according to the second, it goes forward by a hit-and-miss mixture of truth and error.

Our special concern is with the nature of man's being. There is a steady consistency in what the Bible writers say about this, provided that one realizes that terminology used by one writer at one period is not always identical with similar terminology at another period. We shall find ourselves in some difficulty if we always insist in interpreting one word in precisely the same way.

THE SPIRIT OF MAN

This is noteworthy, for example, in the use of the word *spirit*. There is a fundamental consistency in the use of the word, but there are also differences of application.

The key words translated "spirit" are *ruach* and *neshamah* in the Old Testament, and *pneuma* in the New. These words are also used in the sense of "breath" and "wind."

In the Old Testament the fundamental use of *ruach* and *neshamah* is of the principle of life which animates man and the animal world. In the story of man's creation, God breathed into man's nostrils the *neshamah* of life, and thus man became a living being (Gen. 2: 7). As an alternative to the expression "*neshamah* of life" we find "*ruach* of life" in Gen. 6: 17 and 7: 15. In Gen. 7: 22 both words occur together in the phrase, "All in whose nostrils was the breath of life," which reads literally, "The *neshamah* of the *ruach* of life." A study of the usage of the two words can easily be made with such a concordance as Young's Analytical, when their similarity will appear.

This spirit, or breath, is the life-principle which comes from God, and goes back to God, the Lifegiver, when man dies. It is thus an impersonal, vital force, which enables man, a personal being in the image of God, to live as a personal being in a body. The life-principle is found also in animals lower than man (Gen. 7: 15) to enable them to live as physical creatures, though not as personal beings.

At death the body goes to dust, the personal being that has been developing under physical conditions departs to Sheol, or Hades, while the impersonal life-principle, or spirit, goes back to God. This appears from such verses as Psa. 146: 4: "His *ruach* goeth forth, he returneth to his earth" (cp. Psa. 104: 29 of the animals other than man); and also from Eccles. 12: 7: "Then shall the dust return to the earth as it was; and the *ruach* shall return unto God who gave it." In this last passage, as in 3: 21 (R.V.), there is no reference to personal spirit-existence, since the Old Testament teaching is that man as personal being goes at death to Sheol.

We have called this the fundamental use of the term "spirit" in the Old Testament. A similar use of *pneuma* is found in the New Testament in James 2: 26, where the body without the spirit is dead. But *ruach* and *pneuma* have other uses. They are the words used for the Spirit of the Lord, and for other immaterial spirits, such as the angels (*e.g.* Psa. 104: 4; Heb. 1: 7), and evil spirits (*e.g.* I Sam. 16: 14–16; I Tim. 4: 1). The words are fitting for these beings, who, like the wind, are unseen, yet powerful; John 3: 8 is instructive in this connexion: "The *pneuma* bloweth where it listeth, and thou hearest the sound thereof, but canst not tell whence it cometh, and whither it goeth: so is everyone that is born of the Spirit." *Pneuma* is also occasionally applied to man when he has left the body behind at death, and enters upon a non-material existence (Luke 24: 37, 39).

The words are also used of a department, or perhaps aspect, of man's being, in a way that suggests something other than the idea of life-principle. This use is found particularly in Proverbs. While such a phrase as "a faithful spirit" (Prov. 11: 13) need not mean more than a faithful disposition, there are other passages that demand a more precise interpretation, e.g. "The Lord weigheth the spirits" (Prov. 16: 2); "He that ruleth his spirit" (16: 32). There is also the unique use of *neshamah* in this sense in Proverbs 20: 27, "The spirit of man is the candle of the Lord." "Spirit" is never used of the lower animal world in this connexion, so that we are justified in concluding that his possession of spirit *in this sense* marks man off from the other animals.

This use of "spirit" may be connected with the fundamental use, by reason of the fact that it refers to what is unseen and non-material. But there may also be a deeper connexion, which arises from the fact that Scripture speaks of two sorts of life. There is the animal life, sustained by the general life-principle (*ruach*), and there is the new and eternal life, imparted by God over and above the animal life. Ezek. 36: 26, 27 uses the term *ruach* in connexion with this new life, and associates it with the incoming of God's *Ruach*, the Holy Spirit: "A new heart also will I give you, and a new *ruach* will I put into you. . . . And I will put my *Ruach* within you." The same truth emerges in John 3: 6: "That which is born of the *Pneuma* is *pneuma*."

Thus both planes of life need *ruach* or *pneuma* for their existence, and the terms can reasonably be applied both to the seat of the general life-principle in man, and also to the actual or potential seat of the new life-principle, which man alone of the animals can receive. It has been fairly surmised from Scripture that man was originally created as spirit, soul and body, with the spirit, as the God-conscious part, in control of the whole man. At the Fall, the spirit of man dropped out of communion with God, and so the whole man fell into ruin. So long as the spirit is cut off from God and His new life, the whole man is in a state of death. Thus the possession of eternal life depends upon the re-birth of the human spirit by the incoming of the Holy Spirit of life.

Meanwhile there still remains the original central control-house in man, namely the human spirit, which is of very little use until it has been born again. Yet it has an awareness of the mind and body of which it is a part, so that Paul says, "What man knoweth the things of a man, save the spirit of man which is in him?" (I Cor. 2: 11). If the verse already quoted in Prov. 20: 27 is to be referred to the unconverted, as well as to the converted, it means that the seat of inner conviction about certain things as sinful is to be located in the spirit, which acts as the candle of the Lord. But certainly this spirit has no power of regenerating itself; it is not a divine spark that can be fanned into a flame; and until a man has been born again by the Spirit of God, he is "natural" (*psychikos*), and only becomes "spiritual" (*pneumatikos*) at the new birth (1 Cor. 2: 14, 15).

From that time onward it becomes difficult in places in the New Testament to know whether a phrase is to be interpreted of the Holy Spirit or of the regenerated human spirit, and commentators and translators disagree over whether to write a capital before "Spirit" in every place in Rom. 8: 1–13 and even in Gal. 5: 16–25. In cases of doubt it might seem better to retain the capital, so as not to suggest that the regenerated human spirit is capable of sustaining the spiritual life from its own resources. On the other hand, the writing of the small initial letter would convey the important truth that the Holy Spirit comes to transform every part of our being, including the fallen spirit (2 Cor. 7: 1).

To sum up: the word "spirit," as applied to man, may describe (i) that life-principle which man has in common with the animal world; (ii) that which, as the central control point, the individual man has in distinction from the animal world; (iii) that which, when regenerated by the incoming of the Holy Spirit, becomes alive toward God with the life of God, and thus forms the new life-centre of man's being.

"SOUL"

Another important word is the Hebrew *Nephesh*, having a general correspondence with the Greek *Psyche*. It is almost impossible to break away from the frequent translation, *Soul*, but probably there is not a single passage in which some other translation would not be preferable.

The primary sense of the word emerges in the opening chapters of Genesis. In chapter 1 it is used to denote animal life, in contrast to mineral and vegetable existence. In the A.V. and R.V. the word is translated *creature* in vers. 21, 24, and *life* in ver. 30. In chapter 2 it is used of man, but the identity of the word is obscured by the translation in ver. 7, "Man became a *living soul*." The words *living soul* are the same words as have been translated *living creature* in chapter 1. The basic use, then, of *Nephesh* is *Animal being*, and any creatures above the vegetable and mineral order are marked out as *Nephesh*.

There are different orders of *Nephesh*. A man *nephesh* is not the same as a lion *nephesh*. This emerges in Gen. 2: 18–21, when Adam considers all the other sorts of *nephesh*, and finds that while many of them can be domesticated and tamed, not one can be a true companion to him. So God forms Eve as a further human *nephesh* for him.

It follows that a human *nephesh* has all the content of what we

mean by human life. Thus, frequently it is used as the equivalent
of *person*, as, *e.g.* in Gen. 46: 22–27. There is no reason to think
that it means more than this. even in Ezek. 18: 4, "The *soul* that
sinneth, it shall die," *i.e.* the person who sins, he shall die." Further,
it can be used as a synonym for "I," as frequently in the Psalms,
e.g. "My soul waiteth for the Lord," Psa. 130: 5, 6, or "My soul
shall be joyful," 35: 9. The thought is that I myself, as a living
being, wait and rejoice.

But man's animal being is manifested in a material body. It
would probably be true to say that the Bible teaches a unity of man
such as we are only just returning to in our psycho-somatic treatment. We have too long been caught up by ideas of departmentalized man. Man is an animated body, and the animating principle
is the *nephesh*. If we try to localize this animating principle in
man and other animals, it is said to be in the blood, as in Leviticus
17: 11, 14, "The *nephesh* of the flesh is in the blood . . . the *nephesh*
of all flesh is the blood thereof."

There is a profound truth in this statement, going far beyond
what the Hebrews are likely to have understood. But in the
meantime they appreciated that there was a significance in the
shedding of the blood in sacrifice. As it ran in the arteries of the
living body, it had no atoning meaning. But when it was shed in
sacrifice, so that the victim died, then life was given to God as the
equivalent of another life.

This prepared the Jews to understand the meaning of the death
of Jesus Christ. Jesus Christ did not come to a nation, or a religion, that repudiated sacrifice, but to one that had been prepared
for centuries to understand the meaning of His sacrificial death.
So, in pouring out His *nephesh* unto death, and in making His
nephesh an offering for sin (Isa. 53: 10, 12), He was not only offering
His whole being to His Father, but was doing so in a way that
meant the shedding of sacrificial blood. That is why, even though
the terminology is strange to us at first today, we still see that we
are saved through the blood of Jesus Christ, as the New Testament
Christians did. The Bible, in connecting the blood with our salvation, always associates it with the blood poured out in sacrifice,
and not with the blood in the living body. The matter is treated
most ably by A. M. Stibbs in *The Use of the Term "Blood" in Scripture* (I.V.F.). It may be helpful to add that the wine at the Lord's
Supper, as well as the broken bread, must refer us back in symbol
to the death of Christ on the Cross, and not to any risen life that
might be present in the bread and in the wine. Both the form of
the symbols, and the words that the New Testament uses about
them, speak of Christ as He was once upon the Cross, and not of
Christ as He is now.

PERSISTENCE AFTER DEATH

This digression has arisen from the thought that a *nephesh* being has blood (or its equivalent) that sustains the body as long as the *nephesh* is manifested in a body. Life is in the blood cells. At the same time a *nephesh* being is sustained in the body by oxygen which is breathed in from the air. Here we have an interesting link-up with *Ruach* and *Pneuma*, with their meaning of breath and *spirit*. Not all people or animals die through loss of blood. But at death they all cease to breathe. There are, I think, only three passages which actually use an expression which means "breathe out the *nephesh*" at death (Job 11: 20; 31: 39; Jer. 15: 9). But it is clear that something departs at death, and returns again if the body comes back to life. Thus in Gen. 35: 18, Rachel's *nephesh* departs at death, and in I Kings 17: 21, 22, the *nephesh* of the dead child returns in answer to Elijah's prayer.

But what goes out and what returns, and where is it in the meantime? It is difficult to visualize a principle of animal life existing as an independent entity. Yet the Hebrews clearly visualized something as existing. Apart from anything else, the banning of spiritualism proves this. It would have been so easy to dismiss spiritualism on the ground that the departed were extinct, and in fact, this argument is virtually used by some Evangelicals today, who hold a doctrine of non-existence of the soul between death and resurrection. But the dead have an existence in a realm known as Sheol, which, since dead people are buried under the surface of the earth, is commonly spoken of as below the earth. It is true that, being now bodiless, they are deprived of all the activities that are connected with the senses, but they do exist as entities who can be pictured as greeting those who come to join them (Isa. 14: 16; Ezek. 32: 21); and Samuel retains his capacity to foresee the future (I Sam. 28: 19). Jesus Christ also described Abraham, Isaac and Jacob, as still living (Luke 20: 37, 38).

The Old Testament does not say what it is that persists after death, but, if the Hebrew thinker had been pressed, he would probably have used the term *nephesh*. To see why, we must go back in thought to the fact that, though *nephesh* is common to all the animal world, each *nephesh* is manifested according to its kind. A *nephesh* man is a different being from a *nephesh* lion. The most striking difference is that the *nephesh* man is in the likeness of God (Gen. 1: 27), and this likeness must be inward and not outward: otherwise it could be said of apes and monkeys that they too are in the likeness of God. Yet God and angels and other spirit beings are nowhere said to have, or to be, *nephesh*, except merely in a metaphorical sense, as in Lev. 26: 30, where God says, "My *nephesh* shall abhor you."

It must be that the likeness to God consists in man's possession of personality, which involves self-determination, self-awareness, the ability to have ordered fellowship with other personal beings (including God Himself), and presumably the appreciation of goodness, truth, and beauty. These capacities are found in *nephesh* man, as distinct from other *nephesh* animals: but, to judge by the evidence of the Bible, they are found also in God, who is not *nephesh*.

Probably the Hebrew thinkers did not go further than this, and they may not have gone so far. But we are bound to go further, and to note the resemblance between these characteristics in man and what we have seen of the capacities of that mind in man which appears to be more than the physical brain. In other words, these marks of likeness to God lie in the mind, and transcend the purely physical manifestations of *nephesh*, even though they are natural gifts.

It is, however, doubtful whether there is any single Hebrew or Greek word in Scripture to denote this aspect of Mind. In the Old Testament the words *leb* and *lebab* are generally translated *heart*, and occasionally *mind*. In the New Testament *kardia* is translated *heart*, and *nous*, *noema*, *dianoia*, and *phronema* are translated *mind*. Of these latter terms, *noema* and *phronema* are nearer in meaning to thinking, while *dianoia* tends to the idea of *intention*, or *capacity to understand*. The other words, whether translated *heart* or *mind* do not have the sharp distinction that we commonly make, when we contrast comprehending with the mind and loving with the heart. Both words include the rational and emotional sides of man's animal being. There is room for some book on the Biblical conception of thinking. While there is nothing in Scripture that contradicts the discovery of the brain as the centre of thinking, there is no indication that the Hebrew writers were aware of this fact.

But to return to the question of what survives death, according to the Biblical writers. The Old Testament does not specify, but it is a fair deduction that, if pressed for an answer, the answer would be, "*Nephesh* as an organized human personality." In one of its rare references to individuals in the next life, the New Testament uses the equivalent Greek word *psyche* when it speaks of "the souls of them that were slain" (Rev. 6: 9; 20: 4), and the words of Christ in Matt. 10: 28 distinguish between killing the body and killing the *psyche*.

The truth would seem to be, according to Scripture, that personal being survives the death of the body, even though that personal being is incomplete for the time being. We may link this personal being with Mind, if we believe that there is adequate evidence for a Mind that has non-physical properties sufficiently organized to form what can be called a Personal Being. The withdrawal of the spirit, or life-principle, from the body means that the body drops into dust; but the surviving personality must still exist by virtue of the life-principle continuing to sustain it, though now in a different form.

MAN AS A LIVING CREATURE

Let us now try to bring together the Biblical ideas of spirit and animal being, and try to build up our picture of a living man or woman.

The principle of life, or life-stream, is the prerogative of God Himself. It flows from Him continuously, and, when a living creature dies, this life-principle in it is drawn back into the living God. At the beginning this life-principle was put forth to create the universe directly: inasmuch as God is immanent in the universe, this life-principle still runs through all things, even those that we call "inanimate." But in those creatures that we call "animate," the life-principle produces *nephesh*, which in man is a mind-body-personality type of being.

But living creatures are not now created directly by God. They are themselves vehicles for the transmission of the life principle by handing on living cells, which through union are capable of producing a fresh *Nephesh* being. Christians have taken sides over the alternative views of Creationism and Traducianism. According to the former, God creates a fresh soul when the parents beget a fresh body. According to the latter, the parents hand on the soul with the bundle of life that they transmit. The view that has been stated above comes closest to Traducianism, though the soul is not to be visualized as a kind of departmentalized entity. What the parents produce is a personal being, owing its existence to continued contact with the divine life-stream already there in the cells, and capable of developing, both materially through the personal body, and immaterially in mental personality.

Unfortunately every man and woman is infected with the disorganization of sin. Sin does not lie in the body any more than in the mind. It lies in the central maladjustment of the whole being, and in the mental environment of the whole human race. Thus the life-principle, which itself is a neutral force, in the sense that it sustains life in good and bad alike, and does not make men good, is streaming through a self-centred being, although that being was planned to function as wholly God-centred. The Christian speaks of *Original Sin*, and sometimes even of *Original Guilt*. These terms are intended to show that this disorganization of being is not a matter of indifference to God.

CHAPTER XIV

MAN AND GOD

Iɴ the previous chapter we considered the basic structure of man. He is one in whom the life-principle, or energy, of God in creation manifests itself as animal being. In this chapter we we must see how this animal being is related to God, and in particular how it may attain to the knowledge of God.

To see this we must turn to another use of the Biblical term, *spirit* (*ruach* or *pneuma*). Spirit, as breath, is a name for the life-principle. Spirit, as breath, is also the name for the new life-principle. In between there is the use of spirit (as non-material) to denote the non-material central control house of the life. While all animals are *Nephesh*, and all have spirit in the first sense, only man has spirit in the second and third senses. Since the same term, *spirit*, is used of God, and in a special sense of the Third Person of the Trinity, the Holy Spirit, everything leads to the conclusion that the human spirit is the sphere of contact with God, or the spirit world, while at the same time it is the control centre for the whole man.

If the Bible is correct, this spirit may be exercising control, or lack of control, and yet be dead towards God. If it is dead, the man is spoken of as *psychikos*, or *natural* (I Cor. 2: 14, 15). In fact, a contrast is drawn in the New Testament between the natural man with his full quota of animal energies, including the mind, and the spiritual man who has been made alive by the incoming of the Holy Spirit into his spirit. Apart from the passage in I Cor. 2: 14, 15 there is a contrast drawn in Jude 19 between those who are *psychikos* and those who have not (the) spirit. In James 3: 15, wisdom from above is set over against wisdom that is "earthly, *psychikos*, devilish." In Hebrews 4: 12 the Word of God pierces even to the dividing of *Psyche* and *pneuma*. Paul's prayer for the Christians in I Thess. 5: 23 is that their *pneuma*, *psyche*, and body may be preserved entire and without blame at the coming of the Lord Jesus Christ.

There is little doubt that the Bible avoids any suggestion that the animal being (*nephesh*, or *psyche*) can by itself make saving contact with God. Sin and disorganization has brought about a state of death, which is separation from the source of true life, namely God. Hence Jesus Christ came to make it possible for man to

be reborn (John 3) and to pass from death to life here and now
(John 5: 24). For this two things are needed: the forgiveness and
removal of sin, which came about through the atoning and sub-
stitutionary death of Jesus Christ; and the incoming of the new
life of God, which comes through the entering in of the Holy Spirit
to live in the control centre of man's spirit. The two acts can be
separated in theory, but in fact they work together. To seek for
either alone is to miss the blessings that Christ came to bring
(see also p. 24).

The previous paragraph used the term "*saving* contact with God."
This qualification is necessary, since it is obvious, on our previous
theories, that there is a contact with God by virtue of the possession
of the life-principle. We have regarded this principle as something
impersonal. If so, I believe that it has an important bearing on
the experience of mysticism, and in what follows I differ profoundly
from some other writers who have written on psychical research
and similar subjects. In particular one might refer to Raynor C.
Johnson in *The Imprisoned Splendour* (Hodder & Stoughton, 1953).
This is one of the best surveys of the subjects dealt with in this book,
and is full of detailed cases. Nevertheless the conclusion is in
terms of the mystic experience as it emerges in various religions,
and in the ideas that are common to the Eastern mind of the illusion
of separate personality.

Mysticism seeks the experience of Cosmic Consciousness, and
there is a unity of mystic experience in all religions and in none.
The interpretation of the experience largely rests upon the pre-
suppositions of the mystic. If the mystic has no belief in God, the
experience will be interpreted non-theologically, as, for example,
by Richard Jefferies in *The Story of My Heart*. For this reason the
term Cosmic Consciousness is a most happy neutral title.

Essentially mysticism is marked by a sense of oneness. If the
experience is of oneness with God or with the Absolute, there is
commonly the accompanying sense of oneness with all creation.
Individuality may appear to be an illusion. Even God Himself
will frequently be experienced as non-personal, or as All that is.

This unitive state comes to many people as a momentary flash
which is blotted out as quickly as it comes. I have had it myself
on a few rare occasions, and in that flash I have experienced the
unity of all creation. But the more stable mystical experience
comes through an arduous training in prayer and meditation,
accompanied, as in certain forms of Yoga, by physical and mental
exercises. A short cut to some of the mystic experiences is through
certain drugs or anæsthetics. Much prominence has recently been
given to the effects of mescalin in this connexion, following on
Aldous Huxley's book *The Doors of Perception* (Chatto, 1954).

By many people mysticism is regarded as the unifying factor of the religions of the world. Forms of Buddhism and Hinduism are being popularized in the West, and some think that these Eastern forms of religion will supersede Christianity, at least in its dogmatic form. Dogma divides, but mystical experience unites.

Yet Bible Christianity is both dogmatic and experiential, and keeps a sound balance between the two sides. Evangelicalism at its best preserves this balance by its insistence both upon the saving truths of the Gospel and upon the personal experience of Jesus Christ. At its worst Evangelicalism becomes either an insistence upon revealed truths as facts meritorious to be held at all costs, or else a "blessed experience" of something uplifting that changes the life, without any clear ideas about the foundations of the experience.

The striking thing about the New Testament is that it gives no direct encouragement to mysticism as such. Prayer and meditation are there, but they are not accompanied by drastic spiritual and physical exercises. Some are called to a life of poverty or celibacy; others are called to a normal family life and a regular income. But all may know God, and indeed must have a personal experience of Him. The Christian's great delight is to call God by the personal title of "Father" (Rom. 8: 15; Gal. 4: 6). It is probable that to regard God as the all-pervading Absolute was something from which the early Christians felt they had been delivered. Certainly their God was the known, and not the Unknown, God (Acts 17: 23), but the knowledge of Him came to the simplest among them in response to faith.

What, then, is the knowledge of the Absolute to which mysticism attains? The fact that basically mysticism appears to experience God as impersonal makes it likely that the mystic finds Him at the life-force-energy level. It is noteworthy that much of the mystic search is for the God within. The mystic vision may then be a link-up between the conscious mind and the life-force that is normally flowing into the unconscious. This life-force is the impersonal energy of the creative God, and a perception of this force (which is normally unperceived) would pour into the mind an awareness of the basic unity of all life, which is indeed a fact.

This awareness as a fact of perception, and not merely a fact held theoretically, may come as a flash, or may be sustained by the appropriate methods. These methods may vary, but they are directed towards the setting aside of the ordered consciousness with its sense of individuality, so that there may arise an inward awareness of the life-force, and the loss of the individual whole.

Contact with this life-force may also be the source of inspiration in poetry and the arts, as we saw on p. 55 f. If so, the arts are an incipient form of mysticism, and have their attraction because they lift for us in some measure the floodgates of the stream of the life river, so that the words, the music, or the pictures, become dynamic.

If, therefore, the arts are good, mysticism is also good, so long as it does not claim more than its due. It is not the gateway to final truth, but it may be one of the vehicles of expression of Christianity. Indeed, without a plunge into mysticism, Christian devotion is a very dead thing, and may become little more than a display of the bones of orthodoxy. Some of the hymns that are most sung because they are the most helpful, are hymns of mysticism that were not necessarily written by orthodox Christians. One may instance J. G. Whittier's "Dear Lord and Father of mankind," and George Matheson's "O Love, that wilt not let me go." Both of these hymns have that mystic touch about them that springs from the life-force of God.

Mysticism, then, may be the handmaid of Christian truth, but it must not be the master. It is not itself that fellowship with God "in the spirit," of which the New Testament speaks. For the Bible regards this fellowship as based upon the indwelling of the Holy Spirit, e.g. Rom. 8: 9. This is always regarded as something distinct from the immanence of God, which we have connected with the life-principle. The purpose of the incoming of the Holy Spirit into the spirit, or control centre, of man, is to build up the new nature, or the new man (e.g. Eph. 4: 22–24). This new nature is the Christ nature, and Spirit-control is Christ-control. The terms *Old Nature* and *New Nature* need some explanation. The old nature is the organization of the human faculties of man around a wrong centre. The new nature is the organization of the same human faculties around God as the proper centre. It is not some vague entity which is grafted into man when the Holy Spirit comes in.

The process of spiritual growth is the gradual building up of the new creature in Christ (II Cor. 5: 17). There will probably be a series of crises in the course of the period of growth, each marked by a step of surrender to God and fuller trust in Him. That is the value of Christian conventions and conferences. The lethargic Christian is forced to consider areas in his life that are still self-centred, or to learn that victory comes not only through making up the mind to be better, but through intelligent contact with the risen and indwelling Lord Jesus Christ, which is faith. He is brought to the personal application of the Cross, in the sense that he realizes that he has been crucified with Christ (e.g. Gal. 2: 20; Rom. 6: 6), and he comes to see that in Christ there are all blessings for him (e.g. Eph. 1: 3; 2: 6).

Above all, the indwelling of the Spirit means that there is the personal knowledge of the personal God (e.g. John 17: 3). Some Christians are more aware of the presence of God than are others;

some are more expressive in their love for Him: it may well be that temperament plays its part here, for the new nature expresses itself through the same body, using the same emotions and temperament, though the new control centre will direct the emotions from a wrong to a right end. Paul was the same impassioned zealot after his conversion, but now his energies were directed towards building up, and not towards destroying.

All this description is a most inadequate outline of the growth of a Christian through the link with God in his spirit. It is intended as no more than the framework within which the solid building of New Testament truth is to be made, the anatomical chart that is very much less than the living body. Nonetheless it is probably a true basic picture of the underlying New Testament idea of man's growth in the Christian life. It depicts man as a sinner, who constantly needs the forgiveness and cleansing of the sacrifice of Christ, but also depicts him as one who has the new life of Christ emerging in him and transforming him as a practical fact. Holiness is not a fiction.

When does the Holy Spirit come to dwell in the spirit? There are two main schools of Christian thought here. One ties the entrance of the spirit to the moment of conversion, which then is the human counterpart to the Divine regeneration, or new birth. Those who take this view practise Believer's Baptism after the person has made what appears to be a genuine profession of faith in the Lord Jesus Christ as Saviour.

Holders of the other main view believe that it is impossible to date the time when the Holy Spirit comes in, remembering that John the Baptist was filled with the Holy Spirit even from birth (Luke 1: 15). Arguing from such a verse as I Cor. 7: 14, they believe that children of Christian parents have a different status, as being within the covenant of God, and that Christian parents should treat their children, not as prospective prodigal sons, but as Christian children capable of responding to Christian instruction from their earliest days. In this faith they therefore give their children Baptism, which they believe to be the initiatory covenant sign, comparable to Circumcision.

It is not the plan of this book to enter into denominational differences. Having stated the two views, we can point out that the practical question to ask a responsible adult is not, "Have you been baptized (whether as an infant or as a professing Christian)?" but "Have you *now* the saving and sanctifying experience of Jesus Christ?"

THE MEANS OF GRACE

This term refers to the methods by which the Christian life is sustained and advanced. The three basic means are the Bible,

prayer (private and corporate), and the Sacrament of the Lord's
Supper (or Holy Communion).   The indwelling of the Holy Spirit
does not mean that we can be led into the right way by inward
promptings.   This method has been tried, and has frequently ended
in disaster.   The Holy Spirit uses the Bible as His instrument.
The Bible forms the manual of Christian instruction, and in it
Christians have a rule (or Canon, which means Rule) by which
to test all the various "voices" that claim to be revealers of spiritual
truths.   The most mature Christians are those who have read their
Bibles fully and deeply.   Bible truths are not set out in dry packets
that can be handled and taken without effort.   The Bible is a
living Book, whose message can be absorbed only by careful
meditation, and it is best to read it systematically, generally with
the help of some such scheme as the Scripture Union.

Prayer, the second means of grace, is primarily talking to God.
If we include meditation under the first means of grace, prayer
involves praise, thanksgiving, intercession for others, and petition
for ourselves.

It is not irreverent to consider the "mechanics" of prayer.
Why must we pray, and how does prayer effect its results?   It is
fashionable nowadays to say that prayer does not change God's
mind, but changes ours.   This is very much less than a half-truth,
since it obviously can apply only to that one type of prayer in which
it lies in our power to bring about the answer.   Many prayers
concern a much wider field than this.

It is best to say boldly that God has made certain consequences
to depend upon prayer, and, if we do not pray, we do not receive.
An analogy would be to say that it is God's will that I should have
enough to eat, but one means to this end is that I should work.
If I do not work when I have the power to do so God will not feed
me miraculously.   Similarly, if I do not pray, God may withhold
some good thing which He would have given in response to prayer.
It may not be true that prayer changes God's mind, but it is true
that praying forms a channel for God to give.

Moreover, if the Biblical teaching is correct about the spiritual
warfare, prayer is one of the weapons which must be used against
the personal hosts of evil (Eph. 6: 18–20).   Praying in this sense
is as necessary as preaching the gospel; it is a weapon in the same
battle, and it involves wielding the victory of Christ for the over-
throw of His enemies.

There is one other aspect of prayer that is particularly relevant
to some of the themes of this book.   Is prayer the generation of
mind-force that brings about the desired result?   An honest
answer must be, Yes, it can be that.   Dr. F. C. Laubach, the great
missionary pioneer for literacy, has in fact written a booklet on
prayer which maintains this very thing as something normal

(United Soc. for Christian Literature, 1952). There is something exciting and tangible about mind-force prayer. A group of people may come together for a concentrated prayer-meeting, and bring about the desired results. Need they even bring God into the matter at all? Need they even be Christians? The prospect is rather frightening, because we are very close to the borders of magic. C. T. Studd, the pioneer missionary, relates somewhere how a group of medicine-men arrived at one of his meetings determined to stop him from speaking, apparently simply by silent concentration against him. When the time came for him to speak, he had an appalling sense of constraint, and was only able to speak at all after claiming afresh the power of Christ.

Christians are fallible men and women. The promise that "the saints shall judge the world" (I Cor. 6: 2) still belongs to the future! Few of us are competent to decide on what is right and what is wrong for the nations or for individuals. I wonder whether for any single thing we ought to dare to use mind-force prayer. Indeed the New Testament tries to safeguard us against it by directing us to make our prayers *upward* to God (*e.g.* I Tim. 2: 8), and to make them *in the Name of Jesus Christ* (*e.g.* John 15: 16). Prayer, that is, must be vertical, not horizontal, and must be, as it were, filtered through the mediation of Christ. What I will in my own name may be wrong: what I will through Christ will be right.

Yet there is no reason why God should not employ the energy of our own prayers to produce desired results if that is right, just as for certain works of healing Christ may have used the power of suggestion if that was adequate. Autosuggestion may also operate in some of our prayers, and there is nothing derogatory to God in supposing this. If I pray for courage to witness, and receive the courage I desire, does it matter whether God has created a kind of divine courage specially for me, or whether he has drawn out the courage that was already there? People who pray in the Name of Christ find that their prayers are answered, often in an amazing way. Probably, if they concentrated on the mechanism and tried to employ this without praying to God, the results would be pitiably small.

The third means of grace is essentially corporate. It involves the meeting together of God's people to obey the command of the Lord Jesus to eat the broken bread and drink the poured-out wine in remembrance of Him. The symbols speak essentially of violent death, and Christ's own interpretation is that this death was for the remission of sins. It is a means of grace because it brings us back continually to the means of our salvation, which is the death of the Lord Jesus Christ for us. To some the symbols are bare memorials: to others they are effective signs, in the same sense as the Word of God, read and preached, is effective. That

is, the Word of God, given to the senses of hearing, or seeing, is
the guaranteed message of God, and those who trust it find it
effective. Those who merely listen without exercising faith, find
it no more than a set of words. Similarly the bread and wine are
intended to speak to the senses of sight and touch. Those who
trust the meaning, that is there on the guarantee of God, find that
the symbols become effective to them. The Cross is absorbed
into the life. Without faith the bread and wine are no more than
bread and wine. Roman Catholics and some others go much
further than this but it would be beyond the scope of this book to
discuss views which involve some change in, or addition to, the
elements of bread and wine.

One further point may be added about corporate worship.
Here we face the perennial problem of individualism *versus* the
corporate life. If corporate worship is to be judged by the criterion of "What do I get out of it?" the individualist has a perfect
right to stay away and say "I get far more out of my private devotions and meditations." But worship is primarily Godward, and is
the outgoing of the creature to the Creator. Secondarily, corporate
worship is the recognition that we are members of one another,
and "weak" and "strong" alike come together to be linked in the
service of God.

The knowledge of the contact of mind with mind at the unconscious level may be relevant. A group of Christians, intent on
one aim, are probably linked in an effective union, quite apart
from their oneness by virtue of the indwelling of the Holy Spirit
individually and corporately. If there are members whose aim
is different, there will be a loss of power in the Church. That is
why one or two obstinate people in a local church can hinder the
stream of blessing. Their minds are not one with the rest, and
the unified power that should be flowing through the Christian
body is retarded. This is not to belittle the power of the One
Holy Spirit, but, just as the Holy Spirit may be limited in His
working through a wrong attitude of an individual, so He may be
limited through the disordered corporate mind of the Christian
group. Revival means the removal of the corporate obstacles, so
that the mind of the Church is set wholly on Christ and His claims.

There is one danger that may arise through the union of minds
in a corporate body, and that is the undue influence of mass emotion.
Crowd psychology is a study in itself, and one of the classical treat-
ments is K. Trotter's *Instincts of the Herd in Peace and War*. Whether
or not we are right in postulating a group mind for a body of people
who are concentrating on one theme, mass suggestion certainly
operates powerfully on these occasions. The corporate mind may
be swayed to force the group to act as an entity, in a way that
individuals in the group would not act by themselves. A Christian

service may indeed be arranged to exploit this effect. The quiet thinking of individuals is set on one side by the hypnotic effect of the repetition of choruses, and alleluias: the speaker may be spotlighted, and his voice may adopt the tone of a monotonous chant. Individual and mass hypnotism of a mild kind follows. Decisions for Christ made under such conditions may be valueless: on the other hand they may be valuable if the emotional choice is perceived to be the right one and is later ratified by the higher intelligence. A cheering thing about his London and other Crusades in recent years was that Dr. Billy Graham did not make use of hypnotic emotionalism.

CONVERSION

In this chapter the word *Conversion* has been used only rarely. In itself it has many applications, and there are other conversions besides Christian ones. If, however, the view of man that we have set out is true, it will be seen that there are likely to be points of resemblance between Christian and other conversions.

For example, one reads of conversions to Communism after long confinement, or after intensive indoctrination. Some of these conversions are genuine. There can be the breaking down of one mental pattern and its replacement by another. Such a thing is perfectly feasible, and in fact a psychiatrist may often have to produce a conversion in a patient, and rebuild the personality according to a normal pattern.

The fact is that man must be organized around one or more centres. He cannot exist haphazardly. If other things fail, he may obtain temporary unification by dulling the pull of conflicting desires through drink, or drugs, or sex. Conversion is the substitution of one centre for another; and the new central control will affect the orientation of all the faculties. A new dominant idea comes into the human spirit. The difference between a Christian conversion and others is that, not merely an idea, but the Spirit of God Himself comes in to control. An idea of Christian values at the centre is certainly good: but the knowledge and experience of the living God is the only true foundation of Christian experience.

ADDITIONAL NOTE

Other drugs besides mescalin are now being used to release the unconscious. LSD and cannabis, for example, are called *psychedelic*, presumably because they reveal (Greek: *delo*) the psyche. Even if they are not physically addictive, like heroin and cocaine, users become addicted to the experience, which is not integrated into the total personality. Moral stamina and will-power is lessened, whereas inner experience that is grounded in the Spirit of God makes for increased all-round vitality and maturity.

CHAPTER XV

REVELATION AND INSPIRATION

ALL through this book we have referred to the Bible as the inspired revelation of God and His will. We have treated it as absolute truth and assumed that all truths will be in harmony with it. It might seem as though we should have discussed revelation and inspiration much earlier, but it was impossible to do so until we had come to some general understanding of the nature of man and his mind.

We have been able to associate one sort of inspiration with a direct contact with the life-energy that flows through all created being. The poet and artist, by dipping into this stream, are able to clothe their thoughts with a sense of dynamic wholeness that is over and above what is normally perceived. In the Bible there is much of this sort of inspiration, and the Bible, as literature, can stand comparison with other great literature of the world.

But revelation and inspiration in the fuller sense belong, not ultimately to the natural *Nephesh*, but to the spirit of man in communion with the Holy Spirit. This is seen more clearly in prophecy, which is a phenomenon both of the Old and the New Testaments. In view of the evidence available, it may be helpful to begin with the latter. In I Cor. 12–14 Paul writes of prophecy as he knew it in the churches of his day. It is closely connected with Tongues, and, in fact, appears to be an intelligible form of Tongues. Both are said to emerge by way of the human spirit. Thus Paul says that, if he prays in a Tongue, his spirit prays, but his understanding is unfruitful (14: 14). Similarly "the spirits of the prophets are subject to the prophets" (14: 32). Both gifts have their ultimate source in the Holy Spirit (12: 10, 11).

This tallies with the view of man's mind that has been adopted in this book. The Holy Spirit "speaks" at a deep level—in the spirit—and the recipient is aware of this. If he is aware only of something happening, he tries to express himself, but is capable only of unintelligible ecstatic utterances. The inspiration or revelation emerges in a raw form. If, on the other hand, his conscious mind is able to perceive the content of the revelation, he is able to speak out the message as prophecy. This may happen in a sort of ecstasy, or it may be recounted afterwards.

PROPHECY

There is no reason to suppose that New Testament prophecy is of a different order from that which came in Old Testament times. There we find that some of the prophets exhibited marks of supernormal excitement when the Spirit of God came upon them. Saul is the outstanding example, when he stripped off his clothes and fell down before Samuel (I Sam. 19: 23). It is commonly thought by Old Testament scholars that much of the early prophecy by the "sons of the prophets" was of the frenzied type, and that the later prophets discarded such excitement. The evidence for this is not great, and it is significant that the identical word, *Nabi*, is used of the later written prophets and of the earlier prophets also. Ecstasy was probably the normal accompaniment of a prophetic message, and this fact is becoming accepted more and more by scholars today. It was this ecstasy which enabled the Jews to distinguish between a prophet and an ordinary teacher.

In estimating this idea, we must try to rid ourselves of religious ideas which are normally accepted today. If prophecy has ceased today, that is no reason for disputing its existence in the past as a valid method of divine revelation. Nor is it sufficient to give it a psychological explanation, and dismiss it out of hand. The Jews and early Christians were well aware of spurious prophetic ecstasy (*e.g.* Jer. 23; I John 4: 1). But they consistently maintained that there was divinely inspired prophecy which might transcend anything in the prophet's own knowledge.

The ultimate definition of a prophet comes out in an illustrative reference in Exod. 7: 1, 2. Moses complains to God that he is a poor speaker. God replies that He will let Moses be in the position of God, and Aaron be in the position of Moses's prophet. Moses will tell Aaron the words of God, and Aaron will transmit these to Pharaoh. This illustration indicates that a prophet was regarded as receiving the actual message of God and as transmitting it intact. The ultimate essential was to be able to communicate with God. It is in this sense that the patriarchs are given the title of *prophet* (Gen. 20: 7; Psa. 105: 15).

From the Biblical evidence it is clear that God communicates His truth to the prophets in several ways. He may, for example, send a vision, or cause a voice to be heard. These visions and voices could be termed *clairvoyant* or *clairaudient*, in the sense that they were visible and audible to the prophet alone; but they emanated from God, and not from the subconscious mind of the prophet himself. It is impossible to *prove* that any particular prophecy emanated from God: one can only say that the Bible consistently assumes this, that Jesus Christ regards the prophets as truly speaking

the Word of God, and, as a matter of fact, that the Christian
faith is in the succession of the prophetic revelation (*e.g.* Heb. 1: 1;
I Pet. 1: 10–12). The often repeated "Thus saith the Lord" is
to be regarded as a statement of actual fact.

In so-called false prophecy it is likely that the message did not
emanate from God, but either from the prophet's own mind or
from some other spirit being, whom we must regard as an evil
entity. It cannot always have been easy for a listener to judge
whether a prophet was true or false, though two tests are given
in Deut. 13: 1–5 and 18: 20–22. The first test is that of loyalty
to the revealed truth about Jehovah. Even though the prophet
has a gift of precognition, and correctly names a future occurrence
as a sign of his genuineness, he is not to be followed if he urges his
hearers to follow some other god. The second test is that if a
prophet, speaking in the Name of Jehovah, promises a future sign
and this sign does not come to pass, then he is not to be regarded
as genuine.

Obviously these tests were not always applicable. A more
fundamental one is given in Jer. 23: 22, and all the true prophets
of God would agree with this: "If they had stood in my council,
then had they caused my people to hear my words, and had turned
them from their evil way, and from the evil of their doings." False
prophets, like modern fortune tellers, were not concerned with
any moral content in their messages.

It is worth considering why prophecy was revived in New
Testament times, when it had ceased among the Jews. There is
one obvious answer, which is probably the true one. Genuine
prophecy ceased in Israel when there were a sufficient number of
recorded writings for the guidance of God's people. The study
of the Law and knowledge of the Scriptures made fresh revelation
unnecessary. But now God did something new. Jesus Christ
lived, died, rose, and ascended, and a new gospel burst forth on the
basis of these facts of history. Although the early Christians
cherished and studied the Jewish Scriptures, they needed authoritative teaching from God concerning these new facts. So Christ
promised that the Holy Spirit would teach those things which the
disciples could not understand before His death and resurrection
(John 16: 12, 13; 14: 25, 26). He clearly implies that the teachings
which the Spirit will give are as authoritative as His own words.

While the New Testament books were being written and made
generally available, the lack of written authoritative teaching was
met by those who had gifts of prophecy and tongues, as well as
by those teachers who memorized and transmitted what the apostles
themselves taught. This revealed teaching was evidently given
in the Christian services. Prophecy was immediately understand-

Y. M. C. A.

Wiston Lodge,

By Biggar

Lanark-Shire.

27. 1~4

34.8←15   ST. DAVID

112.1~6   ST. MINVER

171   FRENCH

BISHOPTHORPE

able. Tongues were helpful only if someone else present could, as it were, read the message that the speaker was expressing unintelligibly.

If this theory is correct, we should expect that Tongues and prophecy would die out as soon as the New Testament became readily available. This would harmonize with what happened with the Old Testament, and in fact it appears to be what did happen in the Church. Something more will be said about this at the end of this chapter, but the conclusion must be that there is no reason why prophecy and Tongues should exist today, except perhaps in an infant church which does not possess the Scriptures in its own language. An attempt to induce prophecy and Tongues in a Christian assembly in this country would seem to be gratuitous. Those Christians who do have such manifestations are mostly good people, whose minds are stored with Scriptural truth, and therefore what emerges is normally Christian in content. In a prayer meeting that I attended, the Tongues were weird to listen to, and the interpretation that followed was pious, but innocuous. The one prophecy was an exhortation couched in the English of the type used in the Authorized Version. I can imagine that for some people Tongues and prophecy of this sort might be an outlet for neuroses. But the Pentecostalists do such fine work in preaching the Gospel that I do not wish to criticize them on this point.

CONTROL OF THE WRITERS

To return, however, to the Bible itself. Prophecy forms only a part of it, though it covers a wide scope. There are in addition historical records, psalms, and so-called "wisdom writings." They are all within the one volume that our Lord recognized as the inspired Word of God. It is probable, however, that the manner of inspiration for them is different from the more direct form of prophecy.

For the historical records, for example, we can postulate a telepathic control in which God's Mind quietly overruled the minds of the writers and collectors of facts, causing the selection of true and valuable records, and the rejection of what was untrue and not of value for the permanent record that was to comprise the Bible. In the poetical and wisdom writings also one can postulate this controlling Mind, inspiring and blending the thoughts, so that once again literature of permanent value is produced. For some of the poetry at least it is likely that something akin to prophetic inspiration in the spirit is involved.

The moment that one mentions telepathy, it will be objected that, as we have seen, telepathy is very much a hit-and-miss process. If then the Supreme Mind telepathizes its thoughts to the writer,

the possibility is that not all would be received, and those that were
received would be considerably mixed with the personal ideas of
the receiver. An objection of this kind assumes that the Supreme
Mind is something like Dr. Rhine at work at Duke University.
Dr. Rhine's knowledge of the mechanism of telepathy is limited:
but even he knows that some subjects are better than others as
senders and receivers. If he could discover the laws that make
for successful ESP, he could pick those subjects who have the most
reliable ESP capacities. But suppose that in addition he had the
gift of creation, and the capacity to influence the environment and
training of his subjects from the moment of their conception: what
results he could achieve then! God is the Creator and source of
all life. The laws of telepathy are part of His Creation. He can
choose and prepare His subjects, and of such a man as the prophet
Jeremiah He declares that He knew him and set him aside even
before his birth (Jer. 1: 5). Although limited and fallible human
beings were the recipients of revelation, we must not forget the
creative and the controlling power of God all through the life, as
well as the perfect telepathic control that would be possible during
the composing or writing of the records. All this could be done
without reducing the writer to an automaton or violating his free
will.

The Bible is often called the written Word of God, just as Jesus
Christ is the Living Word. The Living Word was manifested in
a human body, and yet the limitations of the humanity did not
obscure the perfection of the Deity. Similarly the human vehicles
of the Written Word did not obscure the perfection of the Divine
message.

To discuss Biblical difficulties would go far beyond the scope
of this chapter. There are no more difficulties in the Bible than in
God's other book of Creation. Such as there are have been har-
monized again and again. The Bible, of course, needs to be read
and applied intelligently: it is not a mere nest of promises to be
dipped into at random. But we are persuaded that the Bible is
indeed the Word of God, and we do not find the need of regarding
it as merely containing the Word of God. Those who wish to
pursue this thought will find my own treatment of it in two book-
lets, *The Authority of the Bible* and *Understanding the Pentateuch*
(Inter-Varsity Fellowship). In this chapter no distinction has been
made between revelation and inspiration. In practice the two are
interlocked. One cannot conceive of an abstract revelation waiting to be received, nor of an inspiration to receive nothing at all.
For those who believe that God can reveal fresh truths to man in
an infallible form, and not merely give flashes of insight to be
worked out in a right or wrong way, the distinction between
revelation and inspiration is merely academic.

It is primarily because of the attitude of Jesus Christ to the Bible of His day that we may accept the full inspiration and accuracy of the Bible. He corrected the rabbis on many of their beliefs, but it is clear from the Gospels that He agreed with them in their belief about the Bible, which was that of full inspiration and accuracy. His immediate followers, who claim to have been instructed by Him, held a similar view, as the Epistles show. Those who criticize Evangelicals for obscurantism and God-dishonouring views of the Old Testament, are, in effect, criticizing the Lord Jesus Christ. He apparently made no distinction between the God of the Old Testament and the Father of whom He spoke.

INSPIRATION TODAY

In John 16: 13 the Lord Jesus Christ promised that the Holy Spirit would guide the disciples into all truth. In the light of similar words in the context, e.g. 14: 26, 15: 26, 27, this promise is most reasonably interpreted as having primary reference to that authoritative teaching that is now to be found in the New Testament. In a secondary sense it can also be taken of the Church down the ages, though experience has shown that it is when the Church has wandered from the Bible under supposed guidance, that it has built up habits of thought and practice that have needed to be reformed. The task of the Christian Church and of individuals in the Church is to take the Bible as the sure and certain revelation of God, and to seek to apply it to our own generation under the guidance of the Holy Spirit. The Christian preacher cannot look for the type of inspiration that would enable him to proclaim some new revelation, but he must try to expound what he finds in Scripture, not confining himself too narrowly to a limited number of themes, but seeking always to bring to light the whole counsel of God. For this he will need the illumination of the Holy Spirit, and his guarantee of accuracy is that his teachings conform to Scripture.

ADDITIONAL NOTE

Speaking with Tongues is now found in some Churches besides the Pentecostal, and I should not like anything in this chapter to cast doubts on the sincerity of those who so speak. The experience has come to dead and formal congregations, especially in the U.S.A., and the sudden influx of life might well produce inexpressible channels of joy. The experience has also been sought by lively Christians, and I am not happy about this, especially when, contrary to anything in the New Testament, hands are laid on them more than once before the gift comes. Some regard private prayer in unintelligible tongues as prayer of a high order, whereas in 1 Cor. 14: 14, 15 Paul says that fruitful prayer is prayer that he and others can understand.

APPENDED NOTE: THE HISTORY OF TONGUES

The history of Tongues after New Testament times is both interesting and puzzling. The early Fathers make few references to the gift, and what they do say is somewhat obscure. In later times there are occasional reports of people who suddenly receive the power to understand and speak foreign languages. Thus St. Francis Xavier (1506–1552) is said to have received the power to converse with the Indians of Travancore, though his own letters do not support this story, since they stress the difficulty that he had in communicating with the people even with the aid of an interpreter.

It is when we come to the close of the seventeenth century that we find the phenomenon of Tongues breaking out among the persecuted Huguenots in the Cevennes. Literally hundreds of young people and children were seized with a kind of ecstasy, during which they preached and exhorted with supernatural fluency. They are commonly referred to as "The Little Prophets of the Cevennes," but we may conveniently consider them here, since they commonly used good French, and not the *patois* that they employed in ordinary conversation.

In 1841–1844 a somewhat similar outbreak of Tongues occurred among young people of between 6 and 16 years of age in Sweden. The onset of the phenomenon was irresistible, and the children preached the need for repentance and the approaching end of the world. When the attack had passed, the person could not remember anything of it.

In Great Britain the phenomenon appeared in the first part of the nineteenth century associated with the Irvingites, later known as the Catholic Apostolic Church. Edward Irving himself, a highly educated man, never received the "gift," much though he desired it, but many of his followers regarded Tongues as the great gift of the Holy Spirit, and Irving often found himself interrupted in his sermons by members of the congregation who spoke in Tongues and prophesied. Irving and his followers eventually made a distinction between the speaking in foreign languages at Pentecost, and the speaking in ecstatic utterances as at Corinth, and they claimed only the latter experience for themselves, though some of their followers earlier had claimed that they were speaking actual foreign languages.

In America Tongues were well known among the Mormons (now known as the Church of Jesus Christ of the Latter Day Saints). Various specimens of their utterances are given by S. Hawthornthwaite in *Adventures among the Mormons*. One sentence runs: "O Me, Sontra Von Te, Par Las A Te Se, Ter Mon Te Roy Ke." On other occasions a few words are virtually repeated: "O, Me, Terrei Te Te-Te-Te."

The Shakers in America often composed hymns in Tongues. D. R. Lamson in *Shakerism As It Is* quotes:

> "O Calivin Christie I No Vole,
> Calivin Christie Liste Um,
> I No Vole Vinin Ne Viste,
> I No Vole Virte Vum."

In the Welsh Revival of 1904–5 it was noted that young people who knew little or no Welsh, prayed fluently in Welsh in public. In the revival which took place in certain parts of India about the same time, Pandita Ramabai testified to the use of various languages in prayer by her women and girls.

There have also been purely secular examples of Tongues. At the end of last century a French lady, whose real identity is hidden under the name Hélène Smith, claimed to have visited Mars in a trance, and spoke and wrote what she claimed to be the Martian language, but which Prof. Flournoy, who published an account of her in a book *From India to the Planet Mars*, claimed to be "a puerile counterfeit of French." Later she claimed to be speaking Hindustani, but although a few of the syllables were Sanscrit, the greater part of them were nonsense. Speaking with Tongues occurs occasionally among those who are under treatment for mental trouble. The patient finds a new language to express the new ideas that are the product of, or sequel to, his unbalanced state.

We have already commented on manifestations of Tongues among the Pentecostalists today. I do not know of any reliable evidence that foreign languages are used by speakers who have never previously had any contact with these languages. There are several stories of missionaries who have attended a meeting in England and heard people speaking blasphemies in some obscure tongue with which the missionary is familiar; but these stories are difficult to track to their source, and stronger evidence is needed before they can be accepted.

I have assumed that Tongues in I Corinthians is an ecstatic utterance rather than a foreign language. When Paul wishes to denote a foreign language, he uses a different Greek word, as in I Cor. 14: 10, 11. This means that Tongues in the Christian congregation are not the same as Tongues on the Day of Pentecost, unless, as some have supposed, the disciples then spoke in ecstatic utterances, while the bystanders received the ability to perceive the meaning in the languages with which they were familiar (Acts 2: 4–6).

In outlining the history of Tongues I have drawn freely upon a book by G. B. Cullen, *Speaking with Tongues* (Yale University Press and Oxford University Press, 1927).

Cullen's own explanation is roughly as follows: In certain meetings there are conditions of external and internal excitement. A person not used to speaking is driven to say something, and may begin to speak normally. As his excitement increases, he is lost for words, and his mind becomes confused and clogged. Rational control vanishes, and the lower centres assume control: there may be partial trance. Without rational control a host of meaningless syllables are produced, which are interpreted as divinely given utterances since they are not the product of the conscious mind.

The Irvingite Movement is dealt with in several biographies of Irving. There is also an excellent chapter in B. B. Warfield's *Miracles: Yesterday and Today* (Reprinted 1953 by Eerdmans, Grand Rapids, Michigan).

An account of the child preachers of Sweden is to be found in Vol. III of *The Prophetic Faith of our Fathers*, by L. E. Froom (Review & Herald, Washington, D.C., 1946). This is an amazing documentary work of the whole history of prophetic interpretation down the ages, to be completed in four large volumes. The author is a Seventh Day Adventist.

CHAPTER XVI

MAN AND HIS FUTURE

VERY many books have been written on the nature of life after death. Most have been speculative in character; for any attempt to write about the future life is bound to be speculative, since so little is said about it in the Bible, especially about the state between death and the resurrection. Therefore this chapter unfortunately also must be speculative.

We have seen that the Bible indicates that the personality of man survives death, and have suggested that this surviving factor is the immaterial mind, which has grown with the body and the brain, and does in fact contain the essence of personality. It carries with it an awareness of all the deeds of the individual while on earth. It is not exactly the storehouse of memories, since this is likely to be the function of the physical brain. But it contains those qualities of transcending time and space that we have seen emerging in certain individuals and at certain times, and consequently it can experience again in a flash any or all of its past life. It is in all probability itself the "book" that will be "opened" at the Judgment Day (Rev. 20: 12).

It seems curious to us that the New Testament does not speak of progress in the intermediate state—so curious that most modern writers do not agree with its silence, but take the idea of progress as a self-evident fact. And yet can a surviving mind of this kind make progress? Its instrument of progress has been left behind on earth. If man here is a soul imprisoned in a body, then release from the body may well be a means to fuller progress. But if man is a body-mind, then mind without body is a crippled form of existence. Death is an enemy, not a friend; even in New Testament times Death is not swallowed up in victory until the very end (I Cor. 15: 26). So long as the personality is without a body, it is still incomplete, and may well be static so far as moral progress is concerned. If a person has lived for the sins of the flesh in this life, does he make progress in the after-life because he no longer has the flesh to tempt him?

Paul realized this in II Cor. 5: 1–10. He first speaks of the wonderful prospect of having a new heavenly body, and he wishes that he could have it now. If he could live to see the Second Coming of Jesus Christ, all would be well: he would at once receive the new clothing. But if he dies before the Second Coming, he will have to pass through a state of being "unclothed." Nevertheless, even that is a desirable state, because he will be at home with the Lord; as he says also in Phil. 1: 23, "to depart and to be with Christ . . . is very much better."

No hint is given that anyone will be able to change his destiny or acquire fuller perfection before the judgment day, and this judgment is always associated with the Coming of Jesus Christ, and not with what follows immediately after the death of the individual. We therefore assume that the surviving mind cannot acquire fresh experiences in any effective sense between the death of the body and resurrection, and Jesus Christ Himself said, "The night cometh when no man can work" (John 9: 4).

The resurrection of the body is a regular part of Biblical doctrine, and it is not so nonsensical as critics sometimes suggest. The earthly body is formed in a remarkable way. We can trace the stages in the process, but cannot say how the process itself is controlled. It is said that all the component parts of our body are renewed over a number of years, and yet there is some principle of identity that persists. Character affects the body, just as the body affects character. The face of a man often takes on a new appearance after conversion. All this is consistent with a moulding of the body by the unseen personality. This must not be pressed to mean that a ready-made personality exists from the beginning; but that in the formation of the body-brain-mind there is a something that is seeking to express itself, i.e. life in a purposive form; life that will make the best that it can of the materials that are fed to it; life that will eventually become conscious personality.

For a period, long or short, after death this personality exists in a static existence. Then suddenly it is granted the power to express itself once more in a body. This body is not the same as the present body, since the Bible speaks of it as "spiritual" and "heavenly" as opposed to "natural" and "earthly" (I Cor. 15: 44, 49). It is, however, such a body as once more constitutes a complete man.

So far we have not attempted to distinguish between the Christian and the non-Christian (or the man who has not been made alive by the incoming of the Holy Spirit). The non-Christian in the intermediate state lacks the means of expression, and yet he is a mind that has only expressed itself hitherto in the material brain and body. Now his Ego experiences the torment that comes from having desires which it cannot express. If the story of Dives and Lazarus is intended as a picture of the intermediate state—and the scene is placed in Hades, not Gehenna (Luke 16: 23)—this is probably the experience of Dives. Although the mind-personality exists, it has certain bounds set to its activity. Thus Dives cannot transfer himself to the happier state that is the other side of a "great gulf" (Luke 16: 26). Nor can he make contacts with other minds on earth (vers. 27, 28). If this is a true picture, it indicates that even the telepathic powers of this mind-personality cannot normally "speak" to those other minds, that are still in the body.

The man whose spirit has been made alive is in a different position. He has begun on earth to express himself Godward through his spirit, and this Godward fellowship continues. So instead of the tortures of non-expression, he has the joy of a closer communion with the Lord. That is why Paul describes even the intermediate state as being with Christ, in a far better way than enjoying His fellowship on earth (Phil. 1: 23), wonderful though that is. In the light of such terms as "rest" and "sleep" which are applied to the departed, it is probable that the intermediate state can best be visualized as a state of quiet rest after the struggles of this life.

How long will this intermediate state continue? The Bible limits it by the Second Coming of Christ. Measured in terms of space-time, this may make the waiting last for very many centuries. But this mind-personality that we have postulated is not subject to time and space as we experience them in the body. There may well be another time scale to which it is subject, though we cannot say what this is. The intermediate state may seem of a very different length when measured by this other scale. In fact it would not be surprising if, for some people at least, the Second Coming seems to follow almost directly after death, because they are now in such a different time-sequence. To me this seems a possible alternative to the view that I have tried to set out, and it would give point to the strong expectations of the first Christians, and even to certain words of Christ, that the Second Coming would occur almost immediately.

When Christ returns, the Bible says that the bodies of those of His people who are alive will be instantly transformed after the pattern of His own risen body (I Cor. 15: 51-53; Phil. 3: 20, 21; I John 3: 2, 3). At the same time the dead in Christ will also rise with renewed bodies (I Cor. 15: 52; I Thess. 4: 16). Since Christ's risen body is an example of the type of body that His people will have, we can gather a few of its properties from the post-Resurrection appearances in the Gospels. This body could be seen, yet could vanish again (Luke 24: 31). It could be touched and could appear as flesh and bones (John 20: 27; Luke 24: 39). It could be sufficiently material to eat food, though apparently food was not a necessity for its continued existence (Luke 24: 41-43).

Since the majority of the bodies of God's people have long since gone to dust, it is obvious that the resurrection body cannot usually be a resuscitation of the old. But it will probably resemble the old in its appearance, since it will again be an expression in a semi-material (?) form of the personality that has grown on earth.

But again we notice a difference between "the resurrection of the just and of the unjust" (Acts 24: 15; John 5: 29). The non-spiritual personality will express itself as it was accustomed to in this life, though the new body may be an even clearer portrayal of its actual character. The spiritually alive personality will form its new body around the Holy Spirit as its centre: it will, in fact, allow the Holy Spirit to express the life of Christ as fully as possible in the new body.

It is necessary to use the qualification "as fully as possible." The Gospel of Christ teaches that one may have salvation and pass from death to life here and now. This is the constant theme of St. John's Gospel. "He that believeth on Jesus Christ is not judged: he that believeth not is judged already, because he has not believed on the name of the only begotten Son of God" (3: 18). "He that heareth my word, and believeth on Him that sent me, hath eternal life, and cometh not into judgment, but hath passed out of death into life" (5: 24). A Christian knows that he is saved, not because of his own works, but because his faith is in what Christ has done.

At the same time the Christian is warned that he will be judged for the use that he has made of his life since conversion (II Cor. 5: 10). The most illuminating passage is probably I Cor. 3: 10–15, where Paul says that Christ is the only foundation for salvation, but everyone must be tested for the building that he does on this foundation. The judgment will be like testing fire. It may burn up all of a man's building, "but he himself shall be saved, yet so as by fire."

This is a hard saying, but it saves us from presumption. At the same time the Gospel message makes us see the tremendous power of the precious blood of Christ. The early Christians knew as well as we do that no man is fit for heaven, but equally they had no doubt that those who lived to see the Second Coming would go instantly to be "for ever with the Lord." (I Thess. 4: 17). There is never a hint of anything like a purgatory, for, as we saw before, if we are not willing to be made fit for God in this life, how should we be made fit merely by having the temptations of the flesh removed? The moment we introduce a purgatory we are back on the level of salvation by works, and the unique message of Christianity, salvation through faith, has been jettisoned in favour of an idea that is common to the general religions and philosophies of the world. Yet a saved Christian may suffer loss. A picture may serve as an analogy for this. When a butterfly or moth emerges from its chrysalis, its wings are no more than little stumps. But during the first half-hour or so these stumps begin to fill out as wings, as the life-giving "blood" flows through them. If, however, the chrysalis has been kept in a small box and the insect has hatched out unnoticed, there will not be room for the wings to fill out entirely. At the end of the set period for expansion, nothing more can be done. The life will flow through the veins so far as it can, but the butterfly will never be able to express its life as fully as it might have done.

The Bible speaks of the post-resurrection life as a time of service and responsibility. For all of us there will be a means of self-expression in the service of God, but, to use the picture that Christ gives in the parables of the pounds and the talents, some will be set over more cities than will others (Luke 19: 11-27; Matt. 25: 14-30). It is no light and easy thing to be a Christian. The greater the privilege, the greater the responsibility. It is in this life that our wings must grow, and the limits of our service hereafter will be set by the flow of the divine life now.

Final Destiny

In one sense, we can say that it would be wonderful if Universalism were true, but the Biblical evidence against it is overwhelming. Some of the strongest words about hell come from the lips of Jesus Christ Himself, and it is only a purely subjective opinion that rejects them as not genuine. We have precisely the same authority for hell as we have for heaven. God is able to destroy both soul and body in hell (Matt. 10: 28). We must be ready to part with anything that may be the cause of casting us into hell (Mark 9: 43-48). The word here is not *Hades*, but *Gehenna*, the burning place for rubbish and filth. The unsaved must go to join the devil in "the eternal fire" (Matt. 25: 46). Their fate is "eternal destruction from the face of the Lord" (II Thess. 1: 9). To be outside of Christ is to be in a state of judgment and death (John 3: 18; 5: 42; I John 5: 12).

Against these terrible statements we cannot set possible universalist interpretations, such as "As in Adam all die, so also in Christ shall all be made alive" (I Cor. 15: 22). It is perfectly true on any interpretation that all who are in Adam die, and all who are in Christ shall be made alive.

It would seem that there are two legitimate beliefs about the destiny of the lost according to the Bible. The orthodox Christian one is that of perpetually continued torment. To man's limited view this may seem inconsistent with the love of God. But our limited view has no idea of what sin really is.

The other interpretation is that, after a longer or shorter time, the lost will be annihilated. Against this it is no argument to say that the adjective "eternal" is applied both to the state of the saved and to the state of the lost, since "eternal life" in the New Testament emphasizes the quality and type of life more than it emphasizes unendingness. The same current of electricity can make a bulb light up, or burn up a man who puts his arms across the cables. It all depends upon how the vehicle of the current is constituted. The eternal fire of God that glows in the saved may be destructive in the lost. There is no text in Scripture which indicates that God cannot annihilate the human personality. But in this controversial matter, it is not the purpose of this chapter to press for a final answer on one side or the other.

Who will be lost? Mercifully the final decision does not rest with us, except that our commission is to preach the Gospel; if it is easy to be saved by remaining in ignorance of the Gospel, it would seem pointless for Christ to stress the urgency of taking the Gospel to the whole world, as He did before His ascension (Matt. 28: 19, 20; Mark 16: 15, 16; Luke 24: 47–49; John 20: 21–23; Acts 1: 8; 26: 17, 18). Surely it would be better to let the many be saved through ignorance, than the comparatively few through faith in Christ? We only know that the Judge of all the earth will do right.

As for the destiny of those who are saved, the pictures at the end of the Book of Revelation give no more than veiled glimpses of the truth. Christ's people will appear as one glorious body through which His life flows unhindered (Eph. 5: 27). The Church is one in, and with, Christ, but it will not be a Nirvana in which individuality is lost. "His servants shall serve Him; and they shall see His face; and His name shall be on their foreheads" (Rev. 22: 3, 4). The life of the individual for the first time will be fully itself, for it will be perfectly integrated to all its fellows in Christ. It will not be lost as the river in the ocean, but will be as the living cell in the living body.

CHAPTER XVII

THE PERFECT MAN

THERE has been only one perfect Man, Jesus Christ. No book on the nature of man could be complete without some consideration of Him, however inadequate such consideration must be. The Christian Church has always regarded Him as both fully God and fully Man, while not professing to understand the mystery of what is technically called the Hypostatic Union.

The Gospel records show that He was truly Man, and no divine apparition . . . He entered the world by the gateway of birth, and passed through the normal stages of growth and development (Luke 2: 52). His body needed to be sustained by ordinary means. He suffered hunger (Luke 4: 2) and thirst (John 19: 28) and often felt the strain of weariness (Mark 4: 38; John 4: 6). Being a man, He experienced the attacks of temptation through various channels (Matt. 4: 1–11), though on no occasion did He fall into sin. Finally He died a real death in fearful agony. There is no doubt that he was Man.

Yet in certain ways He appeared to be more than Man. He claimed for Himself powers which logically belong to God alone. Thus He claimed to have power to forgive sins (Matt. 9: 2 f.; Luke 7: 48 f.) and to be the final Judge of men (Matt. 7: 21 f.; 13: 41; 25: 31; Mark 13: 26, 27). He drew men to Himself in a way that no mere man ought to do, pointing to Himself as the giver of eternal life in response to faith in Himself (John 6: 47, etc.), as the source of comfort and rest (Matt. 11: 28), and as the One without whom no man could come to the Father (John 14: 6) or know the Father (Matt. 11: 27). He claimed that between His Father and Himself there existed a unique union (Matt. 11: 27; John 10: 28, 30). Further He claimed to have had a pre-existence with His Father (John 6: 62; 8: 58; 16: 28; 17: 4, 5, 24).

Proof texts are more precise, though we have not space for all. In John 1: 1 He is the Word and "the Word was God." The Greek does not mean "the Word was divine," as Jehovah's Witnesses assert. In John 20: 28 He accepts the worship of Thomas, when he says "My Lord and my God." In Phil. 2: 6 he is said to have been "in the form of God," where Paul uses a word for *form* that means *essential being*. In Heb. 1: 8 He, as the Son, is addressed as God. In the book of the Revelation He is on the

Throne of God and is worshipped as God (Rev. 5). Moreover there are the well-known words that are so often used at the conclusion of Services, taken from II Cor. 13: 14, "The Grace of the Lord Jesus Christ, and the love of God, and the Communion of the Holy Spirit, be with you all." The position and order of the Names in the sentence would be blasphemous if Christ were not God.

One problem that has vexed the Church is the relation of the Deity to the Manhood during the Incarnation. Some have supposed that Christ emptied Himself of His Deity during His incarnate life, so that He virtually ceased to be God, in fact He came so far under human limitations as to be subject to human errors on points of fact. This is often called the Kenosis theory, the title being taken from the Greek word in Phil. 2: 7 (R.V. "emptied himself"; A.V. "made himself of no reputation").

Yet the New Testament declares that it was while He was upholding all things by the word of His power that He died for our sins (Heb. 1: 3). The reference here is to the divine sustaining of the universe in being, which is ascribed to Christ as the Second Person of the Trinity. So also it is said in Col. 1: 17 "In Him all things consist (or hold together)." To suppose that Christ could virtually cease to be God, suggests for the Christian the impossible conception that the Trinity could become a Duality, and so God is not essentially a Trinity.

But if Christ was God, with the attributes of Godhead while He was on earth, how can His human existence be saved from artificiality? It cannot be solved by assuming two watertight compartments of His being, so that, for example, He did His miracles as God, and ate and slept as Man. Such ideas tend to resolve Christ into two separate persons.

It is probable that the view of man's nature taken in this book has some light to throw on the problem, though I think that only two theologians have attempted this approach. They are W. Sanday in *Christologies, Ancient and Modern* (1910) and *Personality in Christ and in Ourselves* (1911), and W. R. Matthews in *The Problem of Christ in the Twentieth Century* (1952), though in what follows I am not entirely reproducing their views.

The mind of an ordinary man has the two main divisions of conscious and unconscious. The unconscious is the storehouse of memories, and the place of the dynamic urges of life. The unconscious is, as its name suggests, necessarily unknown directly by the conscious mind, but from it come memories and forces that influence the conscious. Fallen men and women have but a poor control of the gateway between conscious and unconscious. Memories and thoughts flash through the gate when they are not wanted, and fail to appear when they are summoned.

But one imagines that a perfect man would have perfect control of the gate. Only those things would flow into consciousness which he desired to admit. Now Jesus Christ was a perfect Man. His divine knowledge and powers were below the threshold of consciousness, and would not flow into His consciousness unless He chose to allow them to do so. While He was on earth He chose to draw only upon human capacities for His daily living. Many of His miracles may have been done because He was perfect Man. Some may have come through the inflowing of His Deity. In His human spirit He held unbroken communion with His Father; He gave the teachings which His Father gave Him to speak (*e.g.* John 8: 47; 14: 10, 24). There were certain things which He was not commissioned to teach, and consequently He did not allow them to flow into His human consciousness. Such was the date of His Second Coming, of which He declares that He, as the incarnate Son is ignorant (Mark 13: 32). Because He was Man His brain and mind needed to grow and develop (Luke 2: 52). Human knowledge which comes piece by piece, is of a different order from divine simultaneous knowledge. One might take as an illustration the knowledge of an architect, who knows the house before a brick is laid, and the knowledge of a labourer, who comes to know the house as he lays brick on brick. In the Incarnation the Architect became the Builder.

The divine function, which Col. 1: 17 and Heb. 1: 3 ascribe to Christ, is that of sustaining the Universe in being. We have spoken of the life-principle flowing through the world, the energy of the creative God, and have seen that this emerges in every man to maintain him in life. May we then be bold enough to hold that in the incarnate Lord this impersonal energy did not flow in alone, but flowed out as well? This energy does not form part of the consciousness of men; nor need it have formed part of the consciousness of Christ. The creative and sustaining work of the universe continued because Christ was still linked to the universe.

Another fact may emerge from the incarnation. We have become aware of a contact of mind with mind at a deep level. There may be something akin to the Collective Unconscious of Jung, linking the human race together. If scientific discovery compelled us to suppose that there were other beings of human status at the time when Adam was created (and I do not think it does), we could still postulate that the whole human race was put "in Adam" by being linked, mind with mind, at a deep level, and that the fall of Adam dragged all others down with him. But at least it is likely that, if there is a group mind of humanity in any sense of the word, it is disordered by sin.

By becoming Man Jesus Christ became linked to this corporate mind of man, or at least telepathically involved with every other man, though He is like the current of fresh water in an ocean of salt. Now we have seen that at this level mind overrides the normal sequence of time, and is in some way linked with what we call past, present and future. How did Christ on the Cross two thousand years ago bear the sins that I have committed today? Could it be that He drew me there in the depths of my personality, with all my sins, and made my sinful personality His own? When Christ died, all humanity died, because He, the second Adam, had involved Himself in the human race, past, present, and future.

Dare we go further? This One who died was the sustainer of the Universe: He was one with it as its source of life. Obviously His Deity did not cease to exist when He died on the Cross, any more than His *Nephesh* ceased to exist. But this suffering on the Cross involved that Creative Energy that sustained the universe, and the agony of His Being was reflected in the strangely darkened sun—the light of the world—and in the earthquake. The centre of the life of the universe suffered human death in that supreme act of atonement and reconciliation, so that Paul can view the atonement as cosmic in its scope. "Through Him to reconcile all things unto Himself, having made peace through the blood of His cross: through Him, I say, whether things upon the earth, or things in the heavens" (Col. 1: 20). And again Paul pictures the whole creation as being delivered, when the sons of God are manifested in their final state of redemption (Rom. 8: 18–25).

What does this mean? We dare not say. It is something beyond imagination. We must, I am certain, stop short of universalism. Everything must be delivered according to its own order of being. New heavens and new earth can arise transformed from the ruins of the old, that are shot through with sin. But men and women are beings who must be saved by deliberate response to God: they are free beings, who may repudiate their place in the redemption of the Cross. But those who come to Christ in repentance and trust come to meet One whom they have met before. They met Him before they had an existence at all. They were there when He was crucified.

BIBLIOGRAPHY

In the text I have included references to a number of books, but readers will realize that many of these are now obtainable only secondhand or through libraries. If I were writing the book again, I should still include them, because they are foundational. Among fresh books, I would mention the following:

PSYCHOLOGY

Freud and the Post-Freudians. J. A. C. Brown. (Pelican)
An Introduction to Jung's Psychology. Frieda Fordham (Pelican)
How the Mind Works. David Cox. (Teach Yourself). Jungian
Alfred Adler. Lewis Way. (Pelican)

EXTRA-SENSORY PERCEPTION

Psychical Research Today. D. G. West. (Pelican)
The Personality of Man. G. N. M. Tyrrell. (Pelican)
The Mind Readers. S. G. Soal & H. T. Bowden. (Faber). Answers to criticisms of this book will be found in the Journal of the Soc. for Psychical Research, Vol. 40. No. 704. June 1960
Probability and Scientific Inference. G. Spencer Brown. (Longmans). See also a long critical review of this by Christopher Scott in the Journal of the Soc. for Psychical Research, Vol. 39. No. 696. June 1958

MIRACLES

Miracles. C. S. Lewis. (Fontana)

OCCULTISM

Exploring the Occult. Douglas Hunt. (Pan). Not from Christian angle.
Christianity or Superstition. Paul Bauer. (Marshall, Morgan & Scott).
Christian Counselling and Occultism. Kurt E. Koch. (Kregel, Grand Rapids, Michigan)

SPIRITUALISM

The Haunting of Borley Rectory. E. J. Dingwall, Kathleen Goldney, Trevor Hall. (Duckworth)
The Spiritualists. Trevor Hall (Duckworth)
These two books show the need to examine evidence that is commonly taken for granted.

Tongues

What about Tongue-Speaking?   A. A. Hoekema.   (Paternoster)
Speaking with Tongues.   Morton T. Kelsey.   (Epworth)
As at the Beginning.   Michael Harper.   (Hodder)

Note: The Journal of the Society for Psychical Research can be purchased by non-members if back numbers are available.   Otherwise public libraries will obtain back volumes on request.

INDEX